D1351745

THE GENTLEMAN'S HANDBOOK

THE ESSENTIAL GUIDE TO BEING A MAN

THE GENTLEMAN'S HANDBOOK

THE ESSENTIAL GUIDE TO BEING A MAN

ALFRED TONG

ILLUSTRATED BY JACK HUGHES

hardie grant books

Contents

Introduction

'A PERFECT GENTLEMAN IS A THING WHICH I CANNOT DEFINE'
ANTHONY TROLLOPE

Are you a gentleman? Am I? I'm not totally sure. Chances are you're not either. I certainly hope I am. You do, too. Don't you?

A perfect gentleman is, indeed, a hard thing to define. It's like trying to describe the feeling of true love or the look of perfect beauty: an almost impossible task. Perhaps that's the point. The very vagueness and mutability of the concept is designed to keep us on our toes, so that we constantly strive to be the very best version of ourselves.

We can be sure of a few things. A gentleman dresses elegantly. He smells nice and takes care of himself and his home. He is confident in all social situations and takes care to put others around him at ease. He is respectful of women – but not too respectful. He is ambitious without being overbearingly so. He is never ostentatious, vulgar or boorish. He is a great wit. In short, he is a total pleasure to be around.

Other aspects are less clear and subject to change. What about the chivalry and selflessness that were once considered hallmarks of the true gentleman? What does that really mean now that most of us are no longer called upon to defend our country and women can hardly be considered the weaker sex?

This book will seek to answer these questions of etiquette, taste and style in all aspects of a man's life. Because while there has never been a definitive expression of what a perfect gentleman is, we all know one when we see one. And it's something we all want to be.

CHAPTER

1

A GENTLEMAN
OF NOTE

A GENTLEMAN IS FOREVER.
AND THESE ARE SOME OF THE FINEST OF ALL TIME

THE MEDIEVAL KNIGHT

The word 'gentleman' dates back to medieval times. 'Gentle' referred to a man who was a member of the gentry. While he was expected to be a brave warrior, a gentleman also lived by a chivalric code of honour. According to a famous poem of the era, 'The Song of Roland', a gentleman strove to 'respect the honour of women', 'refrain from the wanton giving of offence', 'eschew unfairness, meanness and deceit' and 'at all times speak the truth'.

THE RENAISSANCE MAN: BALDASSARE CASTIGLIONE

A gentleman should never appear to be trying too hard. His brilliance should seem effortless and natural. The Renaissance author Baldessare Castiglione called this essential quality, 'sprezzatura'. In *The Book of the Courtier*, a kind of self-help manual for the upwardly mobile Italian aristocrat, he described it as a, 'certain nonchalance, so as to conceal all art and make whatever one does or says appear to be without effort and almost without any thought about it'.

THE REGENCY BUCK: BEAU BRUMMELL

A gentleman is never ostentatious. But it was not always so. Before Beau Brummell, men dressed in clothes that would have made Gianni Versace blush; with lots of gold, filigree, braid and frill. Brummell preferred simple outfits distinguished by their flattering cut, in a sober palette of navy, grey, black and buff. He was a stickler for personal hygiene and insisted on bathing regularly and having his clothes laundered. Both were revolutionary for the time. While Brummell was not of aristocratic birth, he became the acknowledged arbiter of its taste, a power he wielded with great relish. The Prince Regent was said to have burst into tears when Brummell told him his breeches did not fit.

THE VICTORIAN WIT: OSCAR WILDE

Words are the clothes you dress your thoughts in. So a gentleman must be as eloquent as he is elegant. And none were more so than Oscar Wilde. Here was a man who could let his words do the talking. 'A true gentleman is one who is never unintentionally rude', and, 'I am easily satisfied by the very best' are just two of the scores of Wildean maxims that you should live your life by.

THE EDWARDIAN DANDY: THE DUKE OF WINDSOR

While he was undoubtedly one of the most stylish men to ever wear a Savile Row suit, the Duke of Windsor, contributed little else. But his impact on the male wardrobe cannot be ignored. His laidback style was a precursor to the easy elegance of Fred Astaire. Softly tailored suits from Anderson & Shepherd, Fair Isle knits, cuffed trousers, the double-breasted dinner jacket, brown shoes with blue suits, were quite radical at a time when members of the aristocracy still dressed with military precision and formality.

THE MATINÉE IDOL: FRED ASTAIRE

He was neither tall, nor dark, nor particularly handsome. But he was charming, stylish and talented. As a dancer, singer and actor, no one embodied the new, democratic ideal of the gentleman in quite a charming a manner as Fred Astaire. While his clothes were English, he wore them with a grace, fluidity and ease that were all American. Astaire proved that style, charm and talent, not high birth, were the keys to being a gentleman. It was now a club anyone could join. Anyone, that is, willing to put in the effort. In doing so, he allowed all men to dream that one day, a swell gal like Ginger Rogers could be theirs too.

THE JAZZ MAN: MILES DAVIS

How did the great jazzmen of 50s and 60s America respond to the racism and hatred directed towards them? With elegance and style. While the discordant melodies and unpredictable, off balance rhythm of Miles Davis' music was revolutionary, his nonchalant persona and classic Ivy League style was calm and unruffled. What Baldassarre Castiglione called 'sprezzatura', Miles Davis called 'cool'.

THE I-GENT

The gentleman is now a truly democratic, global phenomenon. Whether he's from Tokyo, New York, Milan or Paris, the i-Gent blogs, tweets and updates his Facebook status with the wit and charm of a modern day Oscar Wilde. While he might not wear a suit, he dresses in the latest fashions with an effortless elegance. And he'll show you on Instagram and Tumblr. When it comes to determining taste and etiquette, it's no exaggeration to say that the i-Gent is now more influential than the Prince and the Hollywood star.

UPON
WAKING

A GENTLEMAN IS REVEALED BY HOW HE BEHAVES WHEN THERE IS NO-ONE LOOKING. IS HE WEARING STYLISH PYJAMAS AND A DRESSING GOWN WHEN HE SETTLES DOWN FOR BREAKFAST? IF SO, THEN HE'LL PROBABLY MAKE SURE THAT HE BREAKFASTS WELL. AND THEN YOU CAN BE DOUBLY SURE HE'LL SHAVE PROPERLY, WEAR A NICE FRAGRANCE, COMB HIS HAIR AND SO ON. STYLE BEGINS IN THE MORNING WITH THE NAKED BODY AND ENDS ONLY WHEN YOU GO TO SLEEP.

FIRST THINGS FIRST:

Tea

Tea is important. In a 1946 essay for the London Evening Standard, 'A Nice Cup of Tea', George Orwell wrote, 'Tea is one of the mainstays of civilisation in this country.' According to Orwell and the British, it's almost impossible to get a nice cup of tea outside of Great Britain. So here's how to do it in the proper Orwellian (and British) manner.

1 Loose leaves are better than tea bags. But if you must, always put the bag in first before the water. The water must hit the tea boiling hot in order to release the flavours.

2 Make tea in small quantities, ideally, in a teapot. Tea made in a huge urn tastes horrible and should be avoided. The pot should be made out of china or earthenware.

3   The teapot must be warmed with a splash of boiling water before adding the leaves. You can also preheat your cup if you desire.

4   Tea drinkers like Orwell, liked their tea strong. He recommends six heaped teaspoons of tea per quart of water.

5   Do not imprison the tea in muslin bags, strainers or little steel baskets. The tea must be allowed to circulate freely in the boiling hot water so that all the flavour is released for a full-bodied taste.

6   After making the tea, stir the tea to really get it going and then let it brew for around two minutes. One of the secrets to a good cup of tea is patience.

7   Drink it out of a cylindrical cup that can retain heat, not one of those shallow, open-mouthed cups you get in Starbucks.

8   Used semi-skimmed (reduced-fat) milk. Milk that is too creamy interferes with the flavour of tea.

9   Tea first and then milk. Controversial, yes. Orwell argues that by putting in the tea first, the quantity of milk can then be regulated to the drinker's exact taste.

10   Even more controversial: no sugar. Like beer, tea is a bitter drink. By adding sugar you are no longer drinking tea, but hot sugar water.

COFFEE

A good cup of coffee is more difficult than it looks. Coffee bores go to insane lengths for something called the 'God Shot' a mythical, perfect shot of espresso. You may well have your own technique, but these are the basic principles behind a good cup of coffee.

1 BEANS

Where are they from? Beans from different countries and regions have profoundly different qualities and taste. A decent supplier will be able to talk you through it.

2 FRESHNESS

The date on the tin often refers to when the beans were packaged. What you want to know is the date on which they were roasted or the 'roast date'. Do not buy anything older than 10 days.

3 WATER

Around 98 per cent of a cup of coffee is water. New York has great tap water for coffee, whereas in London tap water should be filtered first. Make sure you have good quality water.

4 STRENGTH

Ask your supplier how much the optimum water to bean ratio per cup is, and strive for a consistent strength.

5 GRINDING

If coffee is over-ground it will taste bitter, and if it is under-ground it will taste thin. Ask your supplier to grind your beans for you. They won't remain as fresh for long, but you can always buy your beans more frequently if necessary.

6 ON DEMAND

Always make small amounts of coffee on demand. Leaving it on a hot plate kills flavour.

7 HEAT

Never add boiling water to coffee. The intense heat will make the coffee bitter and foul-tasting.

8 STORAGE

Keep coffee somewhere dark, dry and cool, in an airtight container. Oxygen and light makes coffee lose its flavour. Experts recommend storing it in the freezer as contact with moisture will cause it to detiriorate.

Breakfast

Even Hunter S. Thompson didn't miss breakfast, calling the meal his 'psychic anchor'. So there is absolutely no reason why you should either.

TOP BREAKFASTS OF TOP PEOPLE

WINSTON CHURCHILL

On his last BOAC flight to the US as Prime Minister, Winston Churchill found that the airline's breakfast menu was not up to scratch. So he wrote one out himself making sure that it contained his customary whiskey and cigar:

> '1st Tray. Poached egg, Toast, Jam, Butter, Coffee and milk, Jug of cold milk, Cold Chicken or Meat. 2nd Tray. Grapefruit, Sugar Bowl, Glass orange squash (ice), Whisky soda.'

Finally, he adds:

> 'Wash hands, cigar.'

PATRICK BATEMAN

Bret Easton Ellis' yuppie psychopath in *American Psycho* has a very specific and creepy breakfast routine:

> '...I eat kiwi fruit and a sliced Japanese apple-pear (they cost four dollars each at

Gristedes)... I take a bran muffin, a decaffeinated herbal tea bag and a box of oat bran cereal... I eat half of the bran muffin after it's been microwaved and lightly covered with a small helping of apple butter. A bowl of oat bran cereal with wheat germ and soy milk follows; another bottle of Evian water and a small cup of decaf tea after that...'

HUNTER S. THOMPSON

Hunter S. Thompson's breakfast was every bit as excessive and hedonistic

as his 'terminally jangled lifestyle':

'Four Bloody Marys, two grapefruits, a pot of coffee, Rangoon crêpes, a half-pound of either sausage, bacon, or corned beef hash with diced chilies, a Spanish omelette or eggs Benedict, a quart of milk, a chopped lemon for random seasoning, and something like a slice of Key lime pie, two margaritas...'

JAMES BOND

Like any true Englishman, James Bond considered breakfast his favourite meal of the day and this is it how it's described in *From Russia with Love*:

'Very strong coffee from De Bry in New Oxford Street, brewed in an American Chemex, of which he drank two large cups, black and without sugar.'

For food he has a boiled egg from a French Marans hen. Toast with

Tiptree Little Scarlet' strawberry jam, Cooper's Vintage Oxford marmalade and Norwegian heather honey from Fortnum & Mason.

BERTIE WOOSTER

P. G. Wodehouse's, Bertie Wooster, on the other hand, is a man of simple tastes. His trusty valet Jeeves always prepares his breakfast for him:

> 'Good morning, sir. I have prepared a breakfast of scrambled egg, kippers and bacon, as per your request.'

> 'Fantastic, Jeeves! I tell you truly, I've worked up a massive appetite and that's no mistake.'

THE FULL ENGLISH

There are plenty of breakfasts like porridge, boiled eggs, brown toast, cereal and yoghurt which release energy slowly, aid digestion, set you up for the day properly and so on. The Full English is unique in that you'll probably want to go straight back to bed after eating one. It's the only breakfast, which is consumed for pure, unalloyed joy. And it's the only meal that can rescue you from a terrible hangover; principally by being so heavy it'll knock you out during the worst phase of it.

ALL IN ONE

Try and do everything in one pan. It's quicker and you won't lose any of the juices. Don't bother with the grill. It's called a 'fry-up' for a reason. Grills are healthier but fry-ups aren't about health. They're about starting the day in the most hedonistic, decadent way possible.

SAUSAGES

Sausages are the cornerstone of any fried breakfast. They take the longest, so get them in first. Try and get a top-quality butcher's pork sausage. Nothing fancy. This will take about 20 minutes on a low heat and when they're nearly done, cut them length ways in half to finish.

EGGS

Next, fry some eggs or scramble them. To scramble, melt a chunk of butter in the pan on a medium to low heat and add the eggs. Get a spatula and break the yolks, but be careful not to mix them up too much. You want the white to be white and the yolk to be yellow. It should take about 2 minutes. Add a little cream if you like. You want it to be moist but not runny.

BACON

In America, they like their bacon so thin and crisp that you can snap it. This absolutely will not do for a Full English breakfast. Get streaky bacon or dry-cured back bacon and put it in the pan. The advantage of pan frying is that you get all the lovely juices, which you can add to your scrambled eggs.

TOMATOES

Get the skin a little crispy by putting them on a high heat for a few minutes. Try and get the tomatoes on the vine, as they're usually firmer and sweeter.

MUSHROOMS

Collapse some field mushrooms in butter on your pan. Large mushrooms should be cut into slices, smaller ones quartered.

FRIED BREAD

Place some slices of bread into the pan to mop up all the cooking juices.

BAKED BEANS

Heinz is best. The baked beans should be cooked last. Cook them until the sauce thickens, so that it doesn't run all over the plate.

SAUCE

HP Sauce or Coleman's Mustard.

TEA

Serve with hot tea (**see page 20**)

THE THIRD WARDROBE

Our clothes are usually split between work and play. There is, however, a third part of a man's wardrobe: the gloriously indulgent clothes he wears at home when only close friends, relatives and lovers are watching.

S acha Rose, managing director of Derek Rose, the London-based pyjama and dressing gown specialist says, 'During the day we dress to please others. These garments are designed purely for relaxation. They are the most comfortable clothes a man can wear. The ultimate indulgence.'

They are also useful on the weekend for picking up milk and bread. And, with the rise of 'freelance' and 'home-working' some lucky gentleman may find themselves in pyjamas and dressing gown well into Monday afternoon.

DRESSING GOWNS

TERRY TOWEL

A terry towel dressing gown taken as a 'souvenir' from a 5-star hotel or exclusive beach resort is the mark of the seasoned traveller. The best are from Claridges in London, the Ritz in Paris and The Plaza in New York. Be warned though: many hotels have cracked down on this, and you may get billed for taking one.

CASHMERE

Derek Rose's 'Duke' dressing gown seems a modest name for such a luxurious garment. Made from the fine, worsted spun cashmere woven by Loro Piana and lined in soft, Italian silk, surely 'King' or 'Emperor' would be more appropriate? You certainly need the fortune of one to afford it.

SILK

Silk dressing gowns are for the ageing lothario. Is it possible to imagine Hugh Hefner without his?

COTTON OR WOOL

For the rest of us, cotton in the summer and wool dressing gowns in the winter will strike an elegant and stylish note at the breakfast table.

PYJAMAS

SILK

Despite the unmistakable whiff of hedonism that follows the silk pyjama, they are in fact, very practical. They wear cool in the summer and warm in the winter,

and being silk, are incredibly soft and comfortable. Get them from a pyjama specialist such as Switzerland's Zimmerli or Derek Rose.

COTTON AND LINEN

There are as many options for striped pyjamas as there are for shirts. In fact, the very best are usually made from soft shirting fabric. All of London's Jermyn Street shirt makers, such as Hilditch & Key, Turnbull & Asser and Emma Willis sell a good cotton and/or linen pyjama. They are also a specialty of Derek Rose.

SLIPPERS

Church's Hercules slipper is probably the most handsome house shoe ever made. You'll see it in Norman Rockwell illustrations of middle-class American life in the 50s and 60s.

Skincare

A man's face is the most expressive part of his body.
Bodybuilders may beg to differ, but hardly anyone has ever
seduced a woman with a flex of the bicep or a flash
of the six-pack, but many have done so with a cheeky smile,
a smouldering look, or a devilishly arched eyebrow.

WHAT KIND OF SKIN DO YOU HAVE?

There are four main types of skin and each requires a slightly different approach for maintenance. To find out what kind of skin you have, wash your face with a soap-free cleanser before bed. The next morning, place a tissue on your face, press hard and take a look.

1. NORMAL SKIN

You have normal skin if the tissue comes away clean. Your skin is not oily, the texture is firm, your pores are small and your complexion is even toned. It's also nice and smooth. Lucky you.

Care: Use a gentle face wash, followed by an alcohol-free toner and a regular moisturiser, day and night.

2. OILY SKIN

The tissue has oily patches all over it. Oily skin becomes shiny and greasy throughout the day and pores are visibly large. This type of skin is prone to blackheads, pimples and other blemishes.

Care: Use a cleanser with salicylic acid to unclog pores and reduce oil production and follow with astringent toner. It's also important to moisturise with a light, oil-free moisturiser during the day.
You can skip moisturising at night, but make sure you have throroughly cleansed and toned before going to bed. If you do get a pimple, do not pick at it as this will not only look unsightly, it will take longer for it to heal.

3. DRY SKIN

If the tissue comes away dry, and your skin is often red, blotchy and easily irritated then you have dry skin. It'll also feel rough to the touch.

Care: Use a mild, soap-free face wash followed by a richer, heavier moisturiser and a weekly hydration mask. Dry skin wrinkles and ages faster than regular skin, so use anti-aging products as soon as possible. Use a gentle face scrub once a week.

4. COMBINATION SKIN

The tissue shows greasy patches but only around the nose, chin and forehead (known as the T-zone). The cheek feels normal and dry.

Care: Requires extra focus on the oily T-zone area when washing and the use of a lighter moisturiser on the T-zone and a heavier regular moisturiser on the test of the face.

SHAVING

Simple steps for a smoother shave and softer skin.

PREP YOUR FACE

Preparation before you start shaving is key. If possible, shave straight after a shower or bath. The moisture will soften the hair and lubricate your skin. Otherwise, use shave oil.

SHAVE CREAM

Avoid those gels that look like ectoplasm. Not only are they often full of ingredients that can irritate your skin, they also smell terrible. Instead, look for unscented shave creams, or ones aimed at sensitive skin.

RUB IT IN

Apply using a circular motion. Coating your stubble with shave cream will help soften it further. Use a brush to make your hair stand on end and easier to shave.

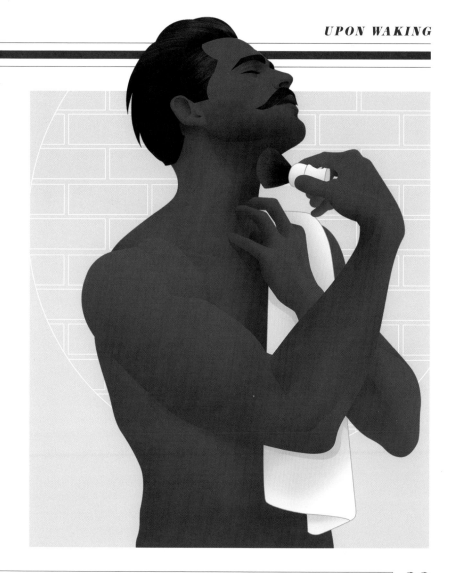

GO WITH THE GRAIN

Shaving against the grain (against the direction in which your hair grows) results in a closer shave, but will also irritate your skin and exacerbate any bumps. So shave your face in the direction that the hair grows, keeping in mind that this changes depending on the part of the face, such as the neck. Everyone is different so if you are unsure, allow your facial hair to grow out for a few days.

SHORT STROKES AND RINSE

Don't copy the Gillette adverts where the guy lets rip right across the whole distance of his face in one swoop. Use short, careful strokes and rinse the blade of your razor regularly. Otherwise, the blades get blocked up and blunt, increasing the likelihood of nicks and cuts.

COLD WATER AND MOISTURISE

Once you have finished shaving, get a face towel, dampen it with cold water and let it rest on your face for a while to close up pores. Moisturise as soon as possible. Shaving puts your skin through a lot of irritation and stress and this helps it recover quickly.

GIVE IT A REST

Try skipping shaving every once in a while, especially at the weekend. It'll be good for your skin.

ELECTRIC RAZOR

Electric razors don't shave as close as a wet shave but they don't irritate your skin as much. Try using a combination of the two, especially if you have sensitive skin.

Beards & Moustaches

Everything you need to know to keep your facial hair in check.

HAPPY BALANCE

With beards and facial hair you're trying to strike a balance. On one hand, anything too artfully sculpted, finessed and 'manscaped' tends to looks stupid. On the other, letting your inner caveman loose with wild and overgrown hair just looks sloppy.

WHAT IS YOUR STYLE?
Sporting a thin Errol Flynn type moustache is unlikely to look good if you dress casually the majority of the time. However, Patrick Grant of the Savile Row tailor, Norton & Sons, shows that a well-groomed beard and a beautifully cut suit go together as well as gin and tonic.

IS THE GROWTH EVEN AND THICK?
Some men simply haven't got what it takes to grow a full beard. A patchy and uneven beard will never look good.

NECK AND CHIN HAIR
There should be no hair on your neck but don't shave it right up to your chin either – you will look as though you have two chins.

SHAPE

The best facial hair for you depends on the shape of your face. A good barber can give you the best advice on the kind that best suits you.

BEARD CARE

KEEP IT CLEAN

A beard or moustache needs to be regularly cleansed. Facial hair is slightly different to the hair on your head. Ask your barber for a specialist cleanser and conditioner.

SCRUB

Facial hair can also lead to a build-up of dry skin and ingrown, hairs requiring the use of a face scrub once or twice a week.

SHAVE AND TRIM

Maintaining your moustache or beard style may require some precision equipment such as a beard trimmer. Stray hairs can be dealt with using a pair of manicure scissors.

CONDITION AND HYDRATE WITH OILS

It's difficult to get standard moisturiser onto the skin as it can get tangled within your beard hair. Facial hair also draws moisture away from the skin. Ask your barber or chemist for advice on moisturising oils.

COMB AND STYLE

You'll need to free your moustache and beard of debris and dry skin with a moustache comb. Combing also ensures that it is kept neat and tidy. Use a wide-toothed comb to tease out any tangles, and alway comb in the direction that your hair grows.

WAX AND SHAPE

Whether you're going for a sleek Errol Flynn look or maybe a caddish Terry Thomas twizzle there are special waxes created for this purpose. Dating back to the Victorian era, beard wax is a useful styling tool and will ensure your beard doesn't look too unruly.

HOW TO GROW A BEARD

1 **START FROM AFRESH**
Start from nothing. Have a proper shave so that the skin is fresh and well treated. This will minimise any early signs of irritation or underlying skin problems.

2 **PERSISTENCE**
Use Jack Black Beard Lube to alleviate any itchiness you might get. The beard will need about three months of growth to reach its full potential.

3 **FIND A SHAPE THAT SUITS YOU**
Different face shapes suit different beards. Ideally, you should go to a professional barber for a consultation. They've seen a million beards on a million men and can tell you the one that suits you best. The temptation is to copy a celebrity or a friend when often that style only really suits them.

4 **PLAY TO YOUR STRENGTHS**
If your beard is patchy in areas you can work with this. Incorporate this into shapes with your barber or even exaggerate patchy spots by using a razor and shaving into the beard (i.e. low cheek lines or a high neck line).

5 **TAKE PRIDE IN YOUR BEARD**
Take care to comb your beard and to give it a regular trim. In addition, visit your barber every two to three weeks to sculpt your beard back into shape.

HAIR

'You're only as good as your last haircut' – **Fran Lebowitz**

I f you're lucky enough to have hair on your head, cherish it, take care of it and run your fingers through it – but not too much. Let girls do that instead. It won't be there forever. After sparkling eyes, a rakishly angled eyebrow, or a dazzling smile, a full head of hair is the most expressive part of a man's presentation.

HOW TO GET A HAIRCUT

Once upon a time a haircut was a process where you plonked yourself down in front of a mirror and a man in a apron would ask, 'The usual, sir?' This man was called a barber. You grunt something like, 'Just a tidy up please' before losing yourself in a copy of *GQ.* Before you knew it, another of life's little chores was over with. It was a bit short perhaps, but who cares? It's hair; it'll grow back. That was before the advent of the stylist, the artiste of hair whose mystical powers could transform you into a sex god with a mere snip, a blow-dry and the application of something called 'product'. But he didn't. He made you look stupid. Follow these steps to end the tyranny of the stylist.

1   **BE CRITICAL**
Take a good look at yourself. Does your haircut match your lifestyle and ambition? Your hair will be a potent symbol of your young and carefree days but remember, those days were

great because you were young and carefree, not because of the overly long hair that brushes up against your shirt collar.

360 DEGREES

2 Look in a three-way mirror or ask someone to take a video with your phone so that you can see right around the back of your head.

RESEARCH

3 Look at magazines and films and begin to form an idea in your head of the kind of haircut you want. Again, be realistic. No haircut will ever transform you into Cary Grant, but if your style is tailored and debonair then that is a good place to start.

CHOOSE (OR CHANGE) YOUR BARBER

4 Always go with a barber of your ethnicity. Thick straight Asian hair requires a different approach to African hair and so on. After

that, think about the general mood and atmosphere. Is it a fashionable hairdresser in an edgy part of town, or a quiet barbershop near your city's financial district? You need someone on your wavelength.

DRESS THE PART

5 If you normally wear a suit they'll give you a haircut geared towards that. A good barber will gauge your haircut based on your style. So dress how you want to look. Don't just wear what was at the foot of your bed on Saturday morning.

SPEAK UP

6 The first cut sets the tone for all the others. Initially, they won't know anything about you. And while it may be tedious, building up a rapport with your hairdresser is vital. What kind of music do you like? The old chestnut – where do you go on holiday? What job do you do? All are vital clues to understanding you and your haircut.

7 GET IT CUT REGULARLY

A man should never look as though he's had a haircut or needs one. In order to avoid this, get your haircut every four to six weeks.

8 BIG EVENT

Don't get a haircut the day before a big event such as a wedding or job interview. Your hair needs at least a week before it looks its best after a haircut.

9 SHORT BACK AND SIDES

After a certain age, say 30, it is perhaps time to settle into some version of short back and sides, the kind of haircut a matinée idol would have sported during Hollywood's golden age. A short back and sides suits almost every face shape and can be worn casually at the weekends and slicked back and smart for the working week.

HAIR MAINTENANCE

WASHING

Strictly speaking you shouldn't wash your hair too frequently as you also wash out its natural grease, which is good for it. If you can, try to restrict it to just a couple of times a week, but definitely no more than once a day.

SHAMPOO AND CONDITIONER

Do use a good quality shampoo and conditioner. Once a week with the conditioner will usually be enough, but more if your hair is long.

STYLING PRODUCTS

Use a matt paste to add texture if your hair is short. Medium-length hair should have a nice flow to it, and this is best achieved by using something gel-based. Long hair doesn't need any product.

HOW TO GO BALD

COMBOVER AND WIGS

Don't. Combovers and wigs are like political scandals - the cover up is worse than the original offence.

SHAVE IT ALL OFF

It's good to do this once you know your barnet is inexorable decline. This way, you won't miss it when it's gone and no one else will either. However, not everyone will have a head that suits a total shave.

HATS

Make a hat a signature part of your look. Just as glasses turn bad eyesight into a stylistic advantage, the right hat, worn correctly, is in many ways, better than a head of hair.

HOLD ON TO WHAT YOU'VE GOT

There are a number of shampoo and conditioning products, which promise to thicken thinning hair and staunch any further losses. Some of them are quite effective. Ask your barber or hairdresser what they recommend.

GROW A BEARD

This will draw attention to your face and away from your head.

HOW TO GO GREY

1 **EMBRACE IT**
Look at Roger Sterling and George Clooney. Both are absolute catnip to women of all ages.

2 **WEAR GREY**
To make the most of your newfound silver fox sex appeal, wear grey and silver coloured clothing near your face. Suits, ties, coats and scarves in shades that are near to your grey colour will help to set it off and highlight it.

3

DYE
If you must, get it done professionally. Home jobs can look harsh and fake.

Again, as with combovers and wigs, the cover up is worse than the crime. A professional colourist will make it look natural.

Fragrance

When shown two sets of short, silent videos – one of men wearing fragrance, one without – researchers at the University of Liverpool, UK, found that women consistently rated men wearing fragrance as more attractive.

The confidence men got from fragrance was reflected in their body language, bearing and movement. It was this psychological boost rather than the smell itself that was making them more attractive to women. Proof, if any more were needed, that fragrance should be a key part of your morning routine. Just not in the way we expected.

WEAR WHAT YOU LIKE
Your fragrance has to please you first. Remember what the research says: it's the impact that the fragrance has on your mood and feeling that's making the girls hot, not just the smell.

MEMORIES
Our sense of smell and memory are closely linked to one another. The

part of the brain responsible for recognising smell, the olfactory bulb, is in the limbic system, which is responsible for memory and emotion. So steer clear of any scents that smell like her father.

GO EASY

Your nose acclimatises to regular smells. What's acceptable to you might be overpowering to others. A woman should only be able to smell it when she goes in for a kiss. Not, say, across a dinner table.

HAVE A WARDROBE

Have a wardrobe of fragrances so that you can match your fragrance with your mood or even the weather. Light citrusy scents work well on hot days. Woody or herbal scents are better for the winter.

BODY CHEMISTRY

Heat intensifies scent, as does oily skin, so use sparingly if your body has these characteristics. However, people with dry and/or cold skin can wear a stronger scent.

THINK ABOUT USING SCENTED PRODUCTS

For a subtle and lasting way of wearing scent, consider shaving creams, body moisturisers and soaps which contain your favourite fragrance. Specialist perfumers such as Floris, Trumper and Czech & Speake all make products scented with their most popular fragrances.

APPLY FIRST, THEN MOISTURISE

Moisturised skin holds fragrance better. Apply first and then use a little fragrance free moisturiser to lock in the scent.

WHERE?

Heat activates and intensifies scent. Body warmth from pulse points like the wrist and neck will help the scent to develop quickly. As will a quick burst after a shower on your chest. Never put aftershave on your face and keep it away from shaved areas – it can cause irritation.

STRUCTURE OF A FRAGRANCE

Like a good glass of wine, a fine fragrance is a complex blend of flavours and aromas, which reveal themselves over a period of time.

TOP NOTES

Citrus and fruit flavours are the inviting smile and hearty handshake of the fragrance: the introduction. This is what you can smell the minute the fragrance is applied. Fruit oils are the most volatile and lively component of a scent and usually short lived.

HEART NOTES

After about 20 minutes or so the lively introduction of the top notes will give way to the heart or middle notes. These woody, floral or spicy ingredients form the main course and are usually more mellow than the top notes. They are what it will predominantly smell of over a period of 2–3 hours. Also called the bouquet.

BASE NOTES

The third element of a fragrance is sometimes known as the 'fond'. This lingers the longest and is what you'll smell on your shirt the day after. Typical base notes include musk, oakmoss oil and vanilla.

STRENGTH

PARFUM

This is the most powerful concentration and typically contains 20–30 per cent of fragrance oil to alcohol. A small dab is usually enough for several hours. It is significantly more expensive, but better value for money.

EAU DE PARFUM

Also pretty strong stuff and composed of 10–20 per cent of oil to alcohol.

EAU DE TOILETTE

Designed to be splashed over the body in the morning, it contains about 4–10 per cent of oil to alcohol.

EAU DE COLOGNE
A lighter mix, eau de cologne contains 3–5 per cent of perfume oil. These are designed to be refreshing and are usually composed of citrus oils. Keep one in the fridge for a quick splash on a hot afternoon. Cologne is usually just applied to fragrances worn by men.

BESPOKE FRAGRANCE: FLORIS

It's hard to imagine a more romantic setting for the creation of a bespoke fragrance than the oak panelled splendour of Floris. Small wonder that everyone from George I to Winston Churchill and James Bond have followed their noses down to number 89 Jermyn Street, London, where this family-run company has been based since 1730.

The process hasn't changed much since Grand Duke Orloff of Russia had his classic 127 crafted for him on the premises, which was later made available to the public. Over a period of 6 months individual scents are tried, tried and then tried again with Floris' perfumer (or nose), currently Sheylagh Foyle.

Gradually the nose begins to discern what it truly loves, free from external influence, and choices are made. Only then does the magic begin, as Sheylagh carefully blends together a mixture that is totally and utterly unique to you. You are then asked to live with this scent for a while, to make sure it is right, before a batch of it is finally made – your own bespoke scent.

STYLE

How To Find Your Style

For a gentleman, dressing well is not a chore or a means to an end, but a great pleasure in and of itself. He needs no excuse or reason to look his best. The benefits of dressing well, such as being more attractive to women, are merely the by-product of good habits ingrained from an early age. And it is never too late to start discovering the joy of good clothes.

WHAT DO YOU LOOK LIKE?

If you're tall and slim then congratulations, most clothes will suit you. Beefcake almost never looks good in a suit. There has never been a stylish rugby player. Fat and/or short? All is not lost. Just look at Al Capone, Scott Schuman, Tony Soprano and Winston Churchill – all men of great panache and style.

A LITTLE BIT OF SCRUFF GOES A LONG WAY

If the shirt collar on your Jermyn Street shirt is a little frayed that's fine. It shows insouciance and character. Likewise, if your tie is a little skew-whiff. The odd, artfully manufactured mistake adds to man's presentation. It is possible to look too manicured and groomed. It's called trying too hard.

WHAT ARE YOU INTO?

What kind of films? What music? Is there an era or design aesthetic that you're drawn to? Beware: don't copy wholesale and choose wisely. For instance, Bryan Ferry channels Cary Grant but never looks like a caricature of him.

WHAT DO YOU WANT TO BE?

Dress for the job you want, not the one you have. Look at the heroes of your profession. Magazine editor? What about Graydon Carter? Business mogul? How about Gianni Agnelli? Go all out. Be the best that you can be. And that means dressing like it.

ONLY FEAR BEING DULL

Diana Vreeland, the legendary editor of *Harper's Bazaar* once said, 'Never fear being vulgar – just boring, middle class or dull'. The biggest crime is to be forgettable. Boring never gets the girl. Charisma or the willing to be different does.

CHARISMA

Got a big pitch at the venture capital firm? Convention will dictate that you wear a suit like all the other boring moneymen. Mark Zuckerberg wore flip-flops and a hoody when he was pitching Facebook. He didn't look particularly elegant, but before speaking even a single word, he demonstrated breathtaking confidence and charisma. And that's the point.

UNDERWEAR

NO
Going commando is uncomfortable, chafing and deviant.

FREEDOM OR RESTRAINT
Underwear is a choice between freedom and restraint i.e. briefs or boxer shorts. Every man has his preference; the choice is yours.

Casual, loose-fitting trousers such as jeans and chinos – boxers. Suits and anything formal where trousers are more fitted – briefs.

RAPPER'S DELIGHT
Only rappers can make a style statement out of their underwear.

DESIGNER
In the song 'Rock Box', Run D.M.C warned against flaunting Calvin Klein underwear. If they couldn't get away with it, neither can you. Keep it subtle and good quality.

BUY YOUR OWN
Mothers, wives or long-term girlfriends buy most of men's underwear for them. Hence the wish-fulfilment-purchasing of David Beckham branded underwear. If you do not want to be compared to this chiselled, handsome man, buy your own.

NO LAUGHING MATTER
Spider-Man boxer shorts will make her laugh. The same goes for thongs and Y-fronts. By all means laugh a woman into bed, but once you're there, the laughing needs to stop.

BESPOKE
Bespoke boxers are the outrageously decadent by-product of the bespoke shirt. The next time you're at the shirt makers, ask them if there is enough excess fabric left over with which to fashion a pair of boxer shorts.

The shirt

THE OXFORD COTTON BUTTON-DOWN SHIRT
Brooks Brothers (aka the Brethren) have been selling the button-down shirt in their flagship store on Madison Avenue, New york, since 1900.

Worn by everyone from JFK to Miles Davis, it is at once classic, conservative and charmingly eccentric.

The golden age of the Brooks Brothers button-down was the 50s and 60s when the shirts were famed for the distinctive fullness and roll of the collar. Get one in blue, white, cream, light pink and blue and white stripe and you'll have the foundation of your shirt wardrobe.

And make sure they're in Oxford cotton. This soft, textured fabric gives the shirt its distinctly casual character and will combine well with almost any kind of knitwear – V-neck, crew neck or cardigan and with casual blazers and sport coats.

The Japanese brand Kamakura, who have just opened a branch in New York, specialise in making button-downs in the manner that Brooks Brothers did in the 50s and 60s. Mercer still make theirs in America out of a very handsome and robust oxford cotton cloth.

Both strive to engineer a collar with that distinctive fullness and roll that gives the button-down its unique character.

SHOULD YOU WEAR A TIE?

There's a school of thought that says you should never wear a tie with a button-down. This is nonsense.

They look great with casual knit ties. If you're a distinguished, older gentleman with a professorial air about you, they even look good with bowties.

HOW TO BUY A SHIRT

GET THE RIGHT SIZE

Know your collar size and arm length. Make sure you can fit one finger between the collar and neck comfortably. Any more and it's too big.

CUFFS

Your cuff should hit the base of your wrist and the root of your thumb. Have at least half an inch of shirt cuff showing underneath your jacket when your arm is by your side. If you can take your shirt off without unbuttoning the cuffs then it is too big.

BUTTON CUFF OR FRENCH CUFF?

Buttons cuffs are casual and sporty. A French or double cuff is where the cuff doubles over and requires a cuff link. This is grander and more formal and better with a suit, but can work perfectly well in a casual smart context.

COLLARS

The collar is the focal point of a shirt. It is designed to frame and draw attention to your face.

COLLAR FIT

The outer edge of the collar should touch the lapel of your jacket. In addition, there should be enough collar to see at least an inch around the side and at the back.

COLLAR WIDTHS

The current fashion is to have collars that are either too small or too large. Small collars don't allow for a decently sized tie knot, leading to comically narrow ties.

Although less prevalent now, try to avoid ostentatious Italian-style collars with two and even three buttons. These will engulf your neck, making you look like a Regency dandy.

As with all things in menswear, it's question of balance.

TIE-LESS

Going without a tie is fine, but requires the right kind of shirt. This is where a robust collar comes into play. Look for one where the ends of the collar stands up on their own up against the lapel of your jacket, not inside, as this looks weak.

THE SEMI-SPREAD

If you are just starting your shirt collection ask for a 'semi-spread' collar. This collar will suit every kind of jacket and is perfect with a classically proportioned four-in-hand tie knot.

THE BODY

Another common mistake is to have shirts either too small or too large. The latter is the most common, with excess fabric billowing out from the body and arms, making it look like a blouse. If your arms and stomach visibly strain under the fabric then your shirt is too small.

COLOUR

THE BLUE SHIRT
Shirts in varying shades and depths of blue flatter every skin colour. If you have blue eyes, wear shirts in as close a shade to your eyes as possible.

THE WHITE SHIRT
Contrary to popular belief the white shirt does not suit everyone. It can give the appearance of 'bleaching' to those with pale complexions, especially, intense shades of 'ice' white. It really works best on darker, tanned complexions. Try cream or slightly softer shades of white if you are fair-skinned.

THE PINK SHIRT
Soft, dusky shades of pink are as flattering as blue. Studies have also found that men who wear pink shirts tend to earn more money than those who do not.

THE POLO SHIRT

A polo shirt is typically a short-sleeved garment (although they can come in long sleeves) made from some kind of knitted fabric, usually pique cotton, with a ribbed collar and a placket containing two or three buttons. René Lacoste used to walk onto court wearing his with a tennis blazer and cream flannel trousers. They are now more commonly dressed down with chinos. Nowadays, they come in all kinds of colours but there is something to be said for sticking with white as René Lacoste did. While pique cotton is the most popular fabric, John Smedley make a very luxurious version in Sea Island cotton.

TROUSERS

JEANS

Get it right and jeans are still one of the sexiest things a man can wear.

THE COLOUR

Always wear them in a deep, dark indigo blue. Black or white jeans are permissible. White is especially useful in the summer and can be used as a neutral counterbalance to the brighter clothes you'll be wearing then. But indigo blue is the original and best.

RAW DENIM

Buy your denim unwashed. They'll feel a bit like cardboard at first but will soften up over time.

FIT

They should fit you as elegantly as any other pair of smart trousers.

That is, slim, but not too slim. And they should sit on your waist, not halfway down your buttocks. Length wise, they should hit the top of your shoe, with little or no break.

TURN-UPS

If you're wearing nice selvedge denim, turn them up once or twice so that the red band on the seam is showing.

STYLE

Keep it simple. Avoid pre-distressed jeans, over-the-top pocket detailing, holes, whiskering, stonewashing, beaching and anything heavily branded.

CARE

Don't wash your jeans – no really. Washing means you'll miss out on the high contrast abrasions, fades and patina that make them totally unique to you. Instead, when they get too dirty put them in the freezer overnight. This will kill bacteria and smells.

IF IN DOUBT

You can pay very little or a lot for a pair of jeans. The choice is bewildering. However, there are really only two brands and two models on the market that are worth considering.

LEVI'S 1947 501XX

There are two types of 501s – the regular kind and the Levi's 1947 501XX. The latter are the Coca-Cola of the denim world – the original and best, worn by everyone from Andy Warhol to James Dean. They feature rigid denim, a slim straight leg and a button fly. Invest in a pair of the 1947 501XX. Although they are a little more expensive, they are totally worth it.

A.P.C. NEW STANDARD

The New Standard from the French brand A. P. C. is devoid of any visible branding, and is the 1947 501XX's sleek, modernist cousin. It's cut slimmer and straighter than the 501.

OTHER TROUSERS

CHINOS

Chinos were popularised by American GIs returning home from WWII. When worn correctly, they impart the glamour, charisma and sex appeal of a demobbed war hero or a member of the Kennedy clan on holiday. Wear them too baggy and you'll look like a dotcom entrepreneur. They should fit like your jeans – slim but not skinny and on your waist. All of the great American outfitters make a great chino: Ralph Lauren, Gant, Brooks Brothers, Dockers – but some of the best come from an Italian company called Incotex.

CORDUROY

There is something about corduroy that reeks of academia and the countryside. Generally speaking the wider the wale (ridges in the fabric) the more professorial and country the look. Narrow wale cords have a younger, more collegiate feel. The British look is to wear them flat fronted, slim and in the colours of the country: fawn, moss green, burgundy red. If you're going for the British look go to Cordings. If you're looking for narrow wale, try Levi's and A.P. C. in cream or blue.

MOLESKIN

The soft, warm handle of moleskin cloth really does feel like mole's skin, hence the name. It is unclear why these hardwearing, colourful trousers are not more popular because they're a great alternative to jeans and go well with all kinds of casual and tailored clothing. At the moment, they remain the preserve of the English country gent who buys his at Cordings of Piccadilly.

GREY FLANNEL

Audrey Hepburn framed a picture of Fred Astaire, whom she adored, in his signature grey flannel trousers. Smarter than cords, chinos or moleskins, you can dress them up for the evening with a dark jacket or wear them during the day with a jumper and a sports jacket. The ultimate combination though is with a blue blazer, white button-down shirt and knit tie.

FLAT-FRONTED OR PLEATED?

Pleats are useful for men who are a bit fuller around the stomach and seat area. The extra cloth allows for more movement and comfort. High-waist, flat-fronted trousers look better on slim men. Pleats are classic and practical, while the flat front is sleeker and probably a little younger and sexier.

CUFF LOVE

Cuffs and turn-ups look good on almost any kind of trouser. Once you start cuffing and turning, it's hard to stop. You'll find that your trousers look a bit unfinished without them. Cuff casual smart trousers such as cords, moleskins and grey flannel. Chinos or any jean-style trousers, such as corduroy jeans, just need to be turned up once or twice.

TROUSER LENGTH

The most common trouser faux pas is to wear them too long, so that fabric pools around the ankle. Trousers play a crucial role in extending the line of the leg and adding height to a man's appearance. They should therefore fall in a straight line before gently gracing the top of your shoe, with little or no break.

KNITWEAR

There was a time when a gentleman had no need for knitted clothing. This kind of hard-wearing, practical and affordable clothing was strictly for the working classes engaged in manual labour. Times changed when knitwear was worn to participate in newly fashionable sports such as polo, cycling, cricket and golf. The word 'sweater' refers to the sweat-inducing properties of wool combined with physical exercise.

THREE FAMOUS CREW-NECK JUMPERS

1 SAINT JAMES BRETON

Saint James is a French company famous for its blue and white striped Breton jumpers. Originally designed for sea fisherman, it is now synonymous with all sea-faring men. The Binic II with its shoulder-fastening detail is the authentic Breton jumper.

2 J. PRESS SHAGGY DOG

Made in Scotland, the charmingly named Shaggy Dog sweater from J. Press is an Ivy League classic. The bright colours they come in are bound to cheer up the mood of anywhere that gets cold and drizzly. They also come in an array of patterns, from Argyle to Fair Isle. 'Shaggy' refers to the extra fuzzy texture of the Shetland wool it's made from. Comfortable, dependable and fun – think of the J Press Shaggy Dog jumper as man's second-best friend.

3 L.L. BEAN NORWEGIAN

The Official Preppy Handbook referred to this iconic piece of knitwear as 'The nearest thing you can get to a prep membership card'. The distinctive blue and white bird's-eye pattern has its origins in Norwegian fisherman's sweaters, and original is still sourced from a manufacturer in Norway.

OTHER JUMPERS

ROLL NECK

The roll neck directs attention to a man's face and is the most dashing piece of knitwear he can own. John Smedley makes a fine merino wool roll neck, which is ideal for layering underneath a sports jacket or blazer. For a rugged roll neck, North Sea Clothing's Submariner was adapted from a design used to keep out the bitter chill of the North Atlantic for sailors on WWII convoys.

CARDIGAN

Despite its military heritage, the cardigan is now definitely a staple of civilian clothing and an urbane one at that.

What was once a genteel item of clothing for the pipe and slippers brigade has evolved into an all-purpose layering piece that can be worn underneath blazers and sport coats.

Use it to add a layer of visual interest to a smart casual ensemble. Never button up all the buttons on a cardigan. Leave a few undone at the top and the bottom for a more nonchalant look.

THE V-NECK

Never wear your V-neck with just a T-shirt or even worse, with nothing underneath. The V is the perfect frame for a shirt, tie and sports jacket. If going without a tie and sports jacket, the collar of a button-down shirt sits pleasingly up against the V.

A navy blazer is one of the most useful garments a man can own. It can be dressed down with a pair of jeans or dressed up with a crisp white shirt, tie and grey flannel trousers. In fact, it will go well with any of the trousers mentioned on page 59. Navy blue suits all skin without the formality of a full suit, making it even more useful. A well cut, two- or three-button navy blazer will make you appear taller and slimmer. (To see how your jacket should fit page 64)

Don't try to use the top half of a blue suit as a navy blazer. No one ever looked good wearing half a

The Blazer

tones and is infinitely more interesting and flattering than black. It serves as a neutral backdrop with which to add bold colour and print, or can provide contrast to muted shades.

Finally, a navy blazer adds a bit of tailored panache to an outfit suit. Get a blazer. All of the great American outfitters make a good one including J. Press, Paul Stuart and Ralph Lauren. Avoid metallic buttons and you'll bring the look up to date. Although there is a certain gin-addled charm to be found with gold buttons.

SUITS

CLOTH AND FIT

Two factors determine how good a suit will look: the quality of the cloth and the elegance of the fit. Everything else – the brand name, number of buttons, colour of the lining, peak or notch lapel – are ultimately vestigial details, important, but not vital. Focus on the following two fundamentals.

ALTERATIONS

When buying your suit, budget for an alterations tailor. No off-the-rack suit will ever fit you perfectly. This should cost 10 per cent of the suit's price.

HOW A SUIT SHOULD FIT

CLASSICAL BEAUTY

A suit is designed to make the body adhere to the classical ideal of male beauty. It should both create the illusion of, and accentuate, broad shoulders, a full chest, a slim waist and long legs. In addition, it's long, clean lines serve the purpose of lengthening the body to create the illusion of height. Bear this in mind when trying on suits.

SHOULDERS

A good suit hugs your shoulders. If the pads extend beyond your shoulders, then it's too big. If it's so tight that your shoulders bulge beyond the padding, then it's too small. A common mistake is to buy a size too big or too small. Always try one up or down, in addition to what you normally take. Different brands have different sizing policies. The shoulder is, in many ways, the focal point of the suit.

THE CHEST
The chest on a good suit has a nice roundness and fullness to it. If the lapels and the cloth around it visibly strain, then the suit is too small. Conversely, it is too big if you can get more than a fist inside.

LENGTH
When you let your arms hang by the side the jacket needs to be long enough to for you to cup the fabric with your hands. This is the length of a classically proportioned suit cut in the British style. The recent fashion has been to cut suits shorter and shorter à la the American designer Thom Browne. Longer is far more flattering.

WAIST
A well-cut jacket has the gently flowing contours of a vintage sports car. It has shape, especially around the waist. Make sure that you can see a bit of daylight in between your arms and the waist.

THE BACK
A suit has three dimensions, so check the back. You're looking for those flowing contours there too. Any bagginess or excess fabric here will need to be eliminated by the alterations tailor. The jacket should fit snugly up against the collar of your shirt. Always look at yourself in a three-way mirror.

SLEEVES
Often men wear decent suits only to let themselves down with sleeves that make them look like Fu Manchu. Sleeves should be slim, but not so slim that your biceps show through. And they need to be short enough to show off a bit of cuff, finishing just at your wristbone.

TROUSERS

In order to accentuate the impression of height, trousers need to create the longest, straightest line possible. This means your trousers will need to sit on your waist and not your buttocks as you may be used to. The waistband should be on your belly button. Good trousers are slim, but certainly not as slim as your jeans and gently grace the top of your shoes. Most men wear their trousers too long so that fabric bunches up around the ankles. This breaks the line we're trying to create.

DOUBLE-BREASTED

The double-breasted is the most overtly masculine of all the suit styles. It's broad lapels and strong shoulders project strength.

THREE-BUTTON

Three-button suits add a slight width to the chest. Only ever do up the middle button. Also, look out for jackets with a roll-over lapel which covers up the top button.

TWO-BUTTON

A two-button jacket is perhaps the most versatile. It's lower stance draws attention to the waist. Never do up the bottom button.

ONE-BUTTON

This is the most dashing and stylish of the suit styles. The single button means that the tailoring must be top notch as there is nothing else to distract the eye. It is sleek.

VENTS

Most jackets come with either one or two vents. The vent-less suit is actually a look with a long and authentic sartorial history. Today, however, it is regarded with suspicion.

PEAK OR NOTCH?

A notch lapel is what you see on most single-breasted suits. A double-breasted jacket must have peaked lapels. On a single-breasted jacket a peak lapel lends a suit a touch of romance and old-world elegance.

WHAT EVERY MAN NEEDS TO KNOW ABOUT TAILORING

Chris Modoo, senior creative at Savile Row brand, Chester Barrie, explains what you need to know when buying a suit:

WHAT TO LOOK FOR IN A GOOD SUIT

◆ Fit is the most important feature.

◆ When trying on a suit wear a good fitting shirt and a proper pair of shoes.

◆ Show plenty of shirt cuff – anything between ½ inch and 1 inch.

◆ There should be no strain of cloth at the front.

◆ The collar of the jacket should fit well into the shirt collar.

◆ Trousers should fit well at the waist and not be too long in the leg.

◆ Proper braces (with buttons) improve the hang of trousers.

◆ If you like turn-ups, have them.

It is completely a matter of personal taste but I prefer deep turn-ups of 2 inches.

◆ A good suit is not flat. It has shape in the chest and a rich, generous sleeve.

Alterations can improve the fit of a ready-made suit, but do not rush into them. Find a good alterations tailor who will carry out quality repairs and adjustments to your clothing.

CARING FOR AND WEARING YOUR SUIT

◆ Avoid using the outside hip pockets on your suit jacket. If they are supplied stitched closed, consider leaving them closed. This will make the jacket last longer.

◆ Do not carry a backpack with a tailored jacket. It destroys the shoulder line and does not look good.

◆ Do not stuff too much in your pockets.

◆ Rotate. Do not wear two days in a row.

◆ Rotate. Do not wear two days in a row.
◆ Brush regularly.
◆ Find a good dry-cleaner but only use sparingly. Twice a year is usually enough.

◆ Do not put too much in your trouser side pockets. It ruins the line.
◆ Wear a pocket square, even when you are not wearing a tie.
◆ Only wear long socks with a suit.

Ties

The tie is the only item of men's clothing whose sole purpose is to make you look good. They serve absolutely no practical purpose. Their purpose is beauty and elegance.

HOW TO TIE A FOUR-IN-HAND

The beauty of the four-in-hand is that no two are ever alike. Its charm lies in its perfectly imperfect asymmetric form. It is both the simplest tie knot and the only one worth knowing.

1 Start with the wide end of the tie hanging about a foot below the narrow end.

2 Cross the wide end over the narrow and turn the wide end back underneath the narrow end.

3 Pass the wide end over the loop you have just created and pull up to the neck. Fuss around with the knot until it looks right to you.

'Bond mistrusted anyone who tied his tie with a Windsor knot. It showed too much vanity. It was often the mark of a cad' – Ian Fleming, *From Russia With Love*.

HARMONY, NOT UNIFORMITY

The colours of your tie should be in harmony with the rest of your outfit, namely, the shirt, jacket and handkerchief. Never exactly match your tie to your handkerchief or to your shirt. Matching all three is trebly bad. Try instead for interesting contrasts of colour and pattern – the look will be both interesting and harmonious.

NEITHER TOO WIDE NOR TOO THIN

Broadly speaking, a tie should correspond to the width of your lapels. Wide lapels, wider tie and vice-versa. The main crime these days is ties that are comically thin. Bankers and football players like to wear theirs too wide and thick.

DIMPLE

A dimple is a nice touch and will come as a natural result of the four-in-hand. You might even try a double dimple, which the Italians call '*la sorchetta*'.

ARCH OUT

Finesse your tie so that it arches out from your collar. That way it looks more alive and fun.

BLADES

There's no need for both blades of your tie to match up. It is perfectly fine for the back blade to be a little longer. Italians sometimes deliberately tie their ties in this way for a freer, more stylish effect.

KEEPER

There's usually loop of fabric at the back of the tie to keep the thinner blade in place. Don't bother. Strike a more carefree note by letting people see the thin end. Twist it round so that it runs parallel even. Putting a tie on needn't mean being uptight.

LENGTH

As a general rule, a tie should hit the top of your waistband. But even so, there is nothing wrong with it being a little short. What doesn't look good is too long.

TIE BARS

What is the point of a tie bar? Can you not use your hand to keep your tie down? And so what if it is flapping around in the wind? As with most men's jewellery, err on the side of caution and discretion.

CASUAL TIES

Knit, wool and linen and silk ties can be used for casual smart outfits, but also to dial down the formality of suits should the mood and occasion require it.

TIE CARE

Because most ties are made of delicate fabrics such as silk, you must be extra careful not to soil them. Never dry clean your ties. Always untie them and then roll them up after wearing them. Don't ever hang them either.

Socks

OVER THE CALF

There's nothing more depressing than a flaccid sock curled around an ankle, revealing two to three inches of pasty leg flesh. Always wear socks which go over the calf.

FORMAL

If you're dressing very formally, wear black socks with a dinner suit and navy with a navy suit. Or you can match them to your trousers.

CASUAL SMART

If you're dressed somewhere in the middle of the formality scale, wear socks in colours, which reference, but not match your shirt, jumper or tie. If you're wearing a suit they can reference but not match the colour of your tie or handkerchief.

FREELANCE

Letting your socks go freelance is slightly more advanced but not that difficult. Make sure the pattern and colour is in the same tone and density of the rest of your outfit. i.e if your wearing a bright blue suit you can get away with bright red socks. If wearing muted tones bright red would stand out too much, perhaps try a burgundy. You want harmony not uniformity.

HARMONY

Socks can come in stripes, polka dots, argyle and in all sorts of colours. The only real rule to follow is that they should not be so loud as to detract attention away from the rest of your outfit. Socks are the finishing touch, not the focal point.

SHOE

After your suit, your shoes are often the most expensive part of your wardrobe and the item that comes under the most scrutiny. Italian shoes tend to be dainty, lightweight affairs. Hand-lasted British shoes from makers such as Church's, Crockett & Jones and Edward Green have the quality that lasts for decades, and the elegance that never goes out of style. In fact, a new pair of British shoes doesn't look anywhere near as good as a pair that has been worn in over a period of years. Alden and Allen Edmonds are two American brands can be mentioned in the same breath as their British cousins.

ESSENTIAL SHOES

There are as many types of shoes as there are people. But these are the four you really need to know.

OXFORD

The Oxford is James Bond's favourite shoe and the epitome of classic, understated and practical English elegance. Black means business – job interviews, big pitches, meeting with the bank manager. Brown is good for almost everything else. Brown suede looks great with grey flannel.

LOAFER

The loafer is the Aston Martin DB7 to the Oxford's Rolls Royce Corniche. It's sleeker, racier but still has elegance and sophistication.

A loafer is a casual smart shoe and generally to be avoided when wearing suit – although some men can make it look good. And although we think of them as an Italian style, a good British loafer from Crockett & Jones is every bit as elegant with the added benefit of being more robust. Gucci loafers in the summer, though, are hard to beat. Wear them with chinos, jeans or flannel trousers. Suede is softer; polished calf leather is sharper.

CHUKKA BOOT

The chukka boot has its origins in the game of polo and has retained its casual, sporty appeal. Do not confuse with the desert boot. Chukka boots are far more elegant and pair well with jeans, corduroy, and moleskin trousers. Never wear with a suit. Chukka boots look great in either calf leather or suede.

BROGUE

A stout country brogue from Trickers can easily perform double duty in the city with jeans and a

Belstaff or Barbour jacket. Don't be fooled by their thick sole – once you've worn them a few times they are eminently comfortable.

SHOE CARE

Good shoes are worth looking after. With a few simple steps they can be made to last decades.

ROTATION

Never wear the same pair of leather shoes two days in a row. Good shoes need time to rest and retain their shape.

SHOETREES

Place your shoes in cedar wood shoetrees as soon as you take them off. The cedar wicks away moisture, helping to prolong the shape and minimise creasing.

DRYING

To dry shoes that have been drenched in the rain, scrunch up some newspaper and place them inside your shoes. Under no circumstances place them near a radiator or use a hairdryer, as this damages the leather.

POLISHING AND CLEANING

Get an old T-shirt and a dab of water to wash away any excess dirt or mud. Then apply a beeswax polish with a separate piece of cloth and shine with a horsehair brush. Finally, give them a once over with the cloth you used to apply the polish with. Repeated polishing over the years gives the leather a character that is far more pleasing than when shop new.

USE A DARKER SHADE

Use a polish that is a shade darker than the original colour of the leather. This helps give your shoes a deeper, richer hue.

REPLACING THE SOLE

Soles will wear away, but this does not mean that the shoes are ready to be thrown away. Ask the shop you bought them from to recommend a cobbler. Under no circumstances go to a rail station repair service or somewhere in a mall. Go to a proper cobbler.

SHOE MOT

Shoes from established manufacturers have a refurbishment service whereby even the shabbiest shoes can be rebuilt to look as good as new.

BLAKEYS

When you first buy a pair of shoes, the tough leather will not be able to bend itself to the stresses your foot puts it under when you walk. This means the front will wear away quicker than the rest of the shoe. A cobbler can place a small metal protector on the front end of the sole called a Blakey to protect against this, saving you the expense of replacing the whole sole.

CHAPTER

4

WORK

THE JOURNEY IN TO WORK

Getting to work via public transport can be trying at the best of times, so it is important to observe the little unwritten rules. This will help make the experience less unpleasant.

STAND ON THE RIGHT; WALK ON THE LEFT

Different countries have different rules. When travelling on escalators on the tube in London, the courtesy is to stand on the right and walk on the left. Ignoring simple rules such as this will expose you as a philistine tourist and hold up hundreds of people behind you.

EXIT FIRST, THEN BOARD

Allow passengers to get off before boarding.

DON'T CROWD AROUND DOOR

Move toward the centre of the train or bus if possible.

GIVE UP YOUR SEAT

Giving up your seat to someone who really needs it is the hallmark of a true gentleman.

DON'T STARE

A little bit of eye contact or even a cheeky smile to the attractive lady sat opposite you is OK. But feasting your eyes on her or anything that seems like staring is creepy.

NEWSPAPERS

For overstretched staff on public transport, free newspapers are a total nuisance. Take yours with you.

BACKPACKS

Not only are backpacks ugly and totally unnecessary, they interfere with the personal space of fellow commuters. If you must have one, wear it on your front during busy times.

TICKET AND MONEY

Have your money ready when waiting to buy a ticket. Have your ticket ready for the ticket barrier.

BE TOLERANT

Just smile politely when the train lurches suddenly and someone is propelled into your personal space. Similarly, if you are the one being propelled, just apologise.

BE CONSIDERATE

Everyone and everything is a little bit more annoying when lots of people are all jammed in together. So think about the volume at which your music is being played; eating, drinking and talking etc. Try to be discreet and create as little fuss as possible.

How to write well

Clarity of writing usually follows clarity of thought. Good writers are prized in almost every profession. In his 1946 essay, 'Politics and the English Language' George Orwell had six elementary rules for good writing.

1. Never use a metaphor, simile or other figure of speech which you are used to seeing in print.

2. Never use a long word where a short one will do.

3. If it is possible to cut a word out, always cut it out.

4. Never use the passive where you can use the active.

5. Never use a foreign phrase, a scientific word, or a jargon word if you can think of an everyday English equivalent.

6. Break any of these rules sooner than say anything outright barbarous.

Writing well doesn't have to be something scary or even very complicated, but the ability to show thought and intelligence in your words will take you a long way. If you want people to read what you write, just follow these five rules:

1 KEEP IT SIMPLE

Write, as anyone would speak in common conversation. Avoid the language of politicians, bureaucrats and marketing people. Simple language often has more impact. Why say 'human rights abuses' when you mean 'torture and murder'? Why say 'hearing impaired' when you mean, 'deaf'? Avoid hackneyed clichés and tired phrases.

2 SHOW AND PERSUADE

If you believe someone is ignorant and stupid then demonstrate how and why. Describe examples of their stupidity in clear and precise language. Don't just tell people they are stupid or you will seem hectoring and arrogant. Use the facts to persuade them. Similarly, if you believe something to be superior explain and show why. Your words need substance. Opinions are good, but only if you have a way of backing them up.

3 DON'T BE A DOUCHE BAG

Avoid congratulating yourself. You're more likely to irritate the reader than impress them.

4 SHORT AND SWEET

'The best way to be boring is to leave nothing out' – Voltaire. Keep your words short and simple. A paragraph is a unit of thought, not of length.

5 CLARITY OF THOUGHT

'A scrupulous writer in every sentence will ask himself at least four questions, thus: What am I trying to say? What words will express it? What image or idiom will make it clearer? Is this image fresh enough to have an effect? And he will probably ask himself two more: Could I put it more shortly. Have I said anything that is avoidably ugly?' – George Orwell

Digital Communication

MOBILE PHONES

If you are inconsiderate, mobile phones can be as annoying as they are useful.

TRY TURNING IT OFF

Whenever possible try turning your phone off rather than putting it on silent or vibrate. It's incredibly charming to give your full attention to whoever and whatever is in front of you.

BLUETOOTH HEADSETS

Bluetooth headsets do not make you look like an FBI agent; they make you look like an idiot. They are however safe and legal when driving and are permissible then, and only then.

IT'S NOT A SIDEARM

So refrain from wearing it on your belt in a holster as though it were a gun. The combination of Bluetooth headset and phone holster must be avoided at all costs.

RING TONES

Comedy ring tones are fun, but if you ever feel embarrassed by your ring tone in the office or at a meeting then it's probably time to change it.

VOLUME

Watch for how loud it is. Unless you're hard of hearing, mid-level volume coupled with the vibrate function is usually enough.

HELLO?! WHAT?!

Do not to disturb others. If the line is bad, do not overcompensate by shouting. Hang up and try again later. Spare us any full-blooded rows and intimate conversations. And respect 'quiet zones' on trains, in hospitals, funeral parlours etc

PEOPLE FIRST, THEN GADGETS

People in your presence take precedence over those on your phone. And that includes butlers, shop staff, waiters, bar staff, bank staff – it is staggeringly rude to be on the phone while ordering food in a restaurant. If you answer a call while getting your hair cut then you deserve whatever punishment your barber decides to give you.

IF IT REALLY IS IMPORTANT

Tell companions, colleagues and guests beforehand that you are expecting an important call. Important in this instance means life and death. When the call arrives, withdraw from the group and take it somewhere private.

NEVER ON THE JOB

Do not take or receive calls in the bathroom, while having sex, or on a first date if you wish to have a second.

TEXT MESSAGES

Text messages can be fun and moreish. To craft or receive a devastatingly witty five-word bon mot is one of modern life's great pleasures. But there are instances when sending a text is wrong.

FACE-TO-FACE
Never communicate important messages by text. Never say anything by text that requires a face-to-face meeting. That includes dumping or sacking someone.

EMOTIONS <3
Do not try to express deep emotions by text, or with emojis or emoticons.

APPOINTMENTS
Never cancel a date or an appointment via text. Always make a phone call.

CONDOLENCES
If you send a message of condolence by text, you may as well not bother.

GRAMMAR
Try not to bamboozle. If the recipient is older try to use conventional language, spelling and grammar. If they're younger, then it can be fun to use emojis, emoticons and txt spk. Just make sure you know what you're doing.

TEXT ALERT
As with ring tones, while comedy text alerts can be fun, they might be embarrassing in a professional context.

SEXTING
Learn the art of sexting on page 162.

EMAIL

Many a glittering career has been derailed with a thoughtless email and careless cc'ing.

DO YOU REALLY NEED TO SEND IT?
Use email sparingly. Never use email when a conversation or phone call will do.

LIMIT YOUR EMAIL USE
Try to limit your email use. Let others know that it is your policy to check and reply to emails three times a day: morning, afternoon

naked though your office, then
you should not send it.
Instead, use the phone or a
clandestine meeting to
communicate anything
private or sensitive. If you
do send an email by
accident get on the phone
immediately to limit the
damage.

EMOTIONS

Think carefully before sending
an email when emotions are
running high. If you really want to
shout at someone, do it over the
phone or even better face-to-face.
Then at least there will be no
permanent record of it. As with
text do not try to communicate
deep emotions such as anger and
love electronically.

and at the end of the day. Constant
emailing can be incredibly
distracting when you're trying
to work.

PRIVACY

There is no such thing as privacy
with emails. Your message can be
stored permanently. If you are not
happy to scream your email at the
top of your lungs whilst walking

SUBJECT LINE

A subject line is like a newspaper
headline. It should briefly sum up
the message the email contains.
A good subject line ensures that
the email will be opened and read.

BCC AND CC

Always use BCC when sending a mail shot. You do not want to expose the recipients to potential e-stalkers. Never use BCC in matters of confidentiality. Instead send a separate email to the third party with a short explanation. Be careful with cc'ing. Try to ensure that everyone cc'd will need or want to read the email.

CAN YOU SEE HOW ANNOYING THIS IS?

Rely on the precise and correct use of language to get your point across. Think about what you want to say and then choose the best words with which to say it. Avoid the use of underlining, **bold**, *italics* or worse: CAPITAL LETTERS. Also, CAPITAL LETTERS IN COLOUR MAKE YOU SOUND LIKE A DEMENTED DRILL SERGEANT.

LEARN HOW TO WRITE A LETTER

No form of electronic communication will ever be as charming, stylish or sophisticated as a handwritten letter. See how to write a letter page 90.

SOCIAL NETWORKS

1 USUAL GOOD MANNERS APPLY

Avoid saying anything you wouldn't in real life. The normal rules of politeness, kindness and respect apply online just as they do in real life. And never ever like your own status updates.

2 WHY WOULD ANYONE CARE?

The tedious minutia of your life is boring, so why share it with the world? Had a jog? Good for you. But no one needs to know the time in which you completed your 5 k run.

3

USE IT SPARINGLY

Constant Tweets and Facebook updates make you look as though you haven't got anything better to do.

4

WILL IT BE OK FOR EVERYONE TO SEE THIS?

Is what you're about to post likely to cause embarrassment to either you or your friends? Is posting a picture of Didier licking the face of a brunette at a party going to endear him to his girlfriend or his 10-year-old cousin?

5

BRAGGING

Today I had breakfast at The Wolseley, lunch at Le Caprice, dinner at J Sheekey before heading off to The Groucho. Oh, did I mention that I'm flying first-class to a tropical island? If you announced all of this to people in a meeting they would rightly think of you as a vulgar braggart. The same rules apply on Facebook or Twitter.

6

EMOTIONS

Emotions are important and best shared with close friends rather than online. Using social networks as an emotional dumping ground does not suit the frivolous and trivial nature of social networking, and will make you appear mentally unstable.

7

IS IT TOO VAGUE?

Will anyone know what you're going on about? Using secret and cryptic language that only a few of your friends will understand is fun but ultimately quite rude.

8

TRY TO BE YOURSELF

Social networks are not a place for personal reinvention. Suddenly becoming more attractive and successful on Facebook and Twitter has the opposite effect, and will instead make you seem desperate and insecure.

HOW TO GET GOOD HANDWRITING

When it's time to communicate something meaningful, a handwritten letter will always feel more personal and heartfelt. In your professional life, a well timed, beautifully handwritten letter sets you apart from the competition. Good handwriting is both seductive and persuasive.

GET THE RIGHT PEN

Get a pen you feel comfortable with. A biro or ballpoint pen will skid across the page too quickly, making your handwriting messy. Consider a fountain pen with the right barrel thickness, speed of ink flow and nib resistance on paper. All of these will make a huge difference.

POSTURE

Sit up straight, with your forearm resting on the table so that the arm moves the fingers not the wrist. Also, make sure your pen is pinched betwixt thumb and forefinger.

IMITATE AND DOODLE

Get hold of examples of writing that you love in a children's handwriting book. Find one that is not dissimilar to your own and analyse each letter. Then you need to doodle and copy it whenever you have the time.

PRACTICE

Practice writing with large letters as this will allow you see where you're going wrong. Doing so will help you get the strokes right before shrinking back down. Avoid the temptation to use your computer and write whenever you can.

STATIONERY

Invest in stationery, paper and notebooks that you love writing on. You'll be that much more inclined to write letters and notes if you have it to hand.

NOTABLE STATIONERY

Jo Irons from London stationers Bureau Direct on essential pen ink and paper.

THE PEN – LAMY 2000

The Lamy 2000 from Germany has a classic fibreglass barrel with platinum coated 14kt gold nib and a piston-operated filling system. It doesn't scream expensive like a Mont Blanc, but just quietly offers style and appeals to those who prefer understatement. Designed by Gerd A. Müller in 1966, the pen still looks modern and writes beautifully.

THE PAPER – RHODIA

The Rhodia brand of stationery has a cult following especially amongst fountain pen users due to the quality of its paper. This stylish French stationery has been around since 1934, so it's really stood the test of time. The distinctive black and orange logo and covers are instantly recognisable and Paul Smith and Francis Ford Coppola are both fans. Look out for notebooks, as well as loose paper.

THE INK – J. HERBIN

Enzo Ferrari famously only used purple for his signature and as technology forces us to use less personal ways of communicating, so the urge to assert our individuality becomes stronger. The J. Herbin brand of ink, which is one of the oldest inks available, was used by Napoleon and Victor Hugo who had a special version made for him to write *Les Misérables.*

Body Language

Good body language plays a vital role in how you present yourself to the world. It can be used to demonstrate confidence, friendliness and even make you more attractive.

HANDSHAKE

A handshake is often the first piece of body language that is used to make a judgment of you. A limp handshake signals weakness; conversely no one wants to have their fingers crushed. A firm handshake consisting of two–three pumps, coupled with a smile and lots of eye contact, is enough.

SMILING

There's no need to smile like a loon. But try and greet everyone you meet with a smile, as this will put them at ease.

POSTURE

Good posture will make you seem taller, slimmer and more confident. It's simple: head high, back straight and shoulders back. But don't overdo it or it'll look militaristic. Always strive to look comfortable and at ease.

SITTING

Sit with your back straight, but not ramrod straight like a sergeant major. You should look comfortable at all times. Some consider the leg cross to be a little effeminate, in which case you might want to try the low cross, where your knees are close together and your legs are crossed at the ankles. Avoid sitting on the edge of a seat or with your legs far apart. Leg shaking and foot tapping when there's no music playing will make you seem nervous.

WALK

Don't drag and shuffle your feet and don't stomp them either. A gentleman is never flustered and always walks at steady, unhurried pace. Watch the movies of Fred Astaire and Cary Grant. Both had an incredibly elegant way of moving and walking.

EYE CONTACT

Meaningful eye contact makes you look sincere and interested in what someone is saying. It's a question of balance. There's a point at which eye contact becomes staring. Unless you're a maniac, your instinct will serve you well here. Try to keep the eye above her shoulder when talking to a woman.

GESTICULATION

In Italy and other Mediterranean countries, hand gestures and movements are a language all of their own. In Northern Europe and America it's best not to overdo it.

FIDGETING

Fidgeting and shaking is a sign of nerves. The most elegant men show great self-possession and economy of movement. Avoid fiddling with your tie, scratching your face or the back of your head.

HOW TO NETWORK

Much of your professional and personal success will come from how good you are at making friends with people.

BE INTERESTED IN OTHERS

'You can make more friends in two months by becoming interested in other people than you can in two years by trying to get other people interested in you.'
– Dale Carnegie, *How to Win Friends and Influence People.*

BE DISCERNING

It doesn't matter how useful someone appears to be, if you don't like them for whatever reason, don't bother trying to cultivate a relationship. It won't work out. The best contacts are the ones you truly like.

FRIENDS FIRST, THEN BUSINESS

Never approach someone new with an agenda. Take the time to cultivate a friendship first. You need to be able to trust each other before you can work together.

REACH OUT FROM A POSITION OF STRENGTH

Even the most successful people have something they would like help with. Find out what this is, and offer assistance. Successful people are always being asked for help. By offering help you are placing yourself in a position of strength.

GO OUT ON YOUR OWN

Networking is a face-to-face business. You need to be visible but not too visible. Don't go to the opening of a crisp packet, but make sure you attend all of the key social and professional events. By going to events on your own, you force yourself to talk to people you don't know.

DIVERSIFY

How many lawyers do you know? How many scientists, fashion designers, politicians, accountants, doctors, journalists, art dealers? Lots of different kinds of friends is not only more interesting, but also more useful to you professionally. You can learn a lot from the friends you make, so the more diverse the group, the better.

MAINTAIN

Catching up for a drink, a quick email, lunch, a phone call, sending thank you notes, birthday cards and making yourself available for people – all of these will make asking for a favour and getting insider information seem natural and easy. Maintaining a contact is harder than making one. Don't become flaky once a contact has been made – you will come across as unreliable and possibly even untrustworthy.

How to Pitch

F or all of it's old-fashioned glamour there is one area in which *Mad Men* is totally relevant to today's gentleman: the pitch. The job interview, the presentation to the bank manager, the hot date you have tonight – these are all pitches. And while you may not be pitching for the Lucky Strike account in a smoke-filled room in Manhattan, the underlying psychology of these potentially life-changing events is the same. You're trying to turn a 'no' into a 'YES'. And that is what Don does best. His name on the door of the ad-agency depends upon it. Here's how.

1 IT'S POETRY NOT PROSE

'A pitch does not take place in the library of the mind, it takes place in the theatre of the heart' Roger Mavity, author, *Life's a Pitch*. There's a scene in *Mad Men* when Don pitches a campaign for a new

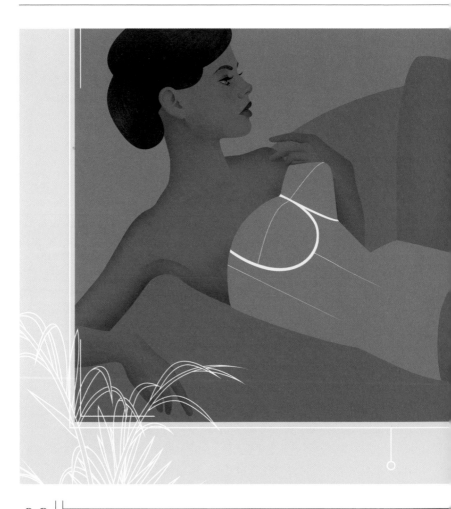

Kodak slide projector called 'The Wheel'. The Kodak executives expected it to be sold as a 'space ship' – the latest in technology. Instead, during the presentation, Don projects a series of his family photos: their wedding day, the births of their children, their birthdays, Christmas. 'This device isn't a spaceship, it's a time machine', he explains. 'It goes backwards, forwards, and takes us to a place where we ache to go again. To a place where we know we are loved. It's not called the Wheel, it's the Carousel.' A final slide reveals the product's new name next to a fairground carousel. The stunned Kodak executives immediately award Don the business.

2 STORY TELLING

The Carousel shows us that a powerful pitch always takes the form of a dramatic and exciting story. All stories have a hero and a problem the hero has to overcome. Tell your story from problem to solution. The problem Don outlined in the Carousel pitch was the power of nostalgia and how we yearn to go back to the past, 'to a place where we know we are loved'. It's not enough to offer consumers the latest technology. The technology must satisfy a deep emotional need, in this case to indulge our love of nostalgia.

3 KEEP IT SIMPLE

Can you sum up your idea with one simple sentence? Don was able to sum his up with one word: 'Carousel'. If you can't do that then either your idea isn't good enough or you haven't thought it through properly. Make brevity and simplicity an obsession. Simplicity not only

demonstrates clarity of thought – vital when millions are at stake – but also confidence.

4 REPEAT YOURSELF

The British Army has a simple mantra for effective communication: 'Say what you're going to say. Say it. Say it again.'

The structure of Don's pitch follows a remarkably similar pattern.

5 POWERPOINT

Don presented his idea using the company's product and he delivered his pitch without the aid of notes. It was as though he was sharing his deepest secrets with his closest confidantes, in the form of an intimate conversation. What he didn't do was fire up a Powerpoint presentation festooned with statistics, arrows, animations and overly long prose which he proceeded to read aloud with no thought for the sanity of the Kodak executives. Use Powerpoint like Don used the Carousel – primarily for pictures and maybe add a few simple slides containing short, powerful sentences that move your story along. Powerpoint can be powerful, but only if you use it sparingly.

THE ART OF CONVERSATION

ALWAYS SAY LESS THAN NECESSARY

The person that speaks least and listens most is always considered the best conversationalist. This means you have to indulge the opposite party, no matter how boring they are. On the flip side, you get to enjoy another person's company when they are fascinating and funny.

AVOID UNNECESSARY DETAILS

As with writing, keep your stories short and sweet. Describe the details only when they move the plot along or add some vital bit of colour or humour. Make sure there is a hero, a plot and a satisfying ending or punch line.

DON'T ALWAYS TALK ABOUT YOURSELF

Build others up too. Tell stories where your friends are the heroes.

ASK QUESTIONS AND LISTEN TO THE ANSWERS

Don't fire off a volley of questions before giving the other person a chance to answer properly. Don't interrupt. Listen to their answer and perhaps ask a follow-up question or say something that builds on what they said.

DON'T BE A KNOW IT ALL

There's no need to bring up every single inaccuracy in someone's story, especially if it's not important. And often when you contradict someone, it's just an excuse to butt in.

YOU DON'T HAVE TO AGREE WITH EVERYTHING THEY SAY

A good-natured difference of opinion is one of the hallmarks of civilisation. It also shows confidence. But never let it get personal or heated.

FIND A SUBJECT THEY WANT TO TALK ABOUT

Again, this is about being a good listener and being able to coax out a subject that gets them excited and animated. It also shows you are interested in what they have to say, as well as wanting to know more about what they are interested in. A conversation should be a two-way street.

LISTEN

Try to be genuinely interested. This can be hard sometimes, but it is the most vital skill of a good conversationalist.

EYE CONTACT

Eye contact is very important. It shows that you are actually engaged in what the other person has to say. See page 94 for tips on eye contact.

Office Politics

TOXIC OFFICE PERSONALITIES

According to Oliver James, author of *Office Politics: How to Thrive in a World of Lying, Backstabbing and Dirty Tricks*, there are three main types of toxic personalities that you need to keep an eye out for in the modern workplace. You could be sharing an office with one of these people right now.

1 THE MACHIAVEL

The Machiavel treats offices politics not as fact of life or a chore, but as a sport to be enjoyed and played with relish. Throughout history we see examples of positive Machiavels like Ghandi and Mandela. These are individuals who used their political skills for the greater good. Your office Machiavel plays games in order to further their own self-interest.

WHAT TO DO
This person will say almost anything about you behind your back. The way to deal with Machiavel is to understand that they will tell the most outrageous lies about you in order to further their own interests. Then you can begin to make sense of what you're dealing with.

2 THE PSYCHOPATH

According to James, the psychopath, will use the death of colleague's parent or close relative as an opportunity to manipulate that person to their benefit or advantage. You or I might show empathy. Not the psychopath, who'll be thinking 'How can I benefit?'

WHAT TO DO
James recommends putting as much space between you and the psychopath as possible. There is simply no way you can do business together. He will always betray you.

3 THE NARCISSIST

These are the easiest to spot. They're always talking themselves up. Their surface confidence and grandiosity is merely a mask to conceal feelings of worthlessness and powerlessness. The most successful are able to convert these feelings of inadequacy into charm and glamour.

WHAT TO DO
Just praise them. They respond easily to flattery. But do it indirectly through a colleague so that it seems more sincere.

SOCIALISING

How to go out all night

FOOD

Treat food like fuel and snack occasionally. A full-blown dinner will make you tired.

HAVE A RUN-UP

Start with an aperitif like a Negroni or Aperol Spritz which are designed to whet the appetite. Always begin with light drinks before progressing to the heavy stuff.

DON'T JUST SIT THERE

If you just sit there and drink you'll fall asleep. Stay engaged. Have a dance! Chat up a girl! Have fun!

STAY HYDRATED

A glass of water between each drink will help you stay sober and prevent you from possibly looking foolish. It will also make all the difference the next day!

TACTICAL ORDERING

Americans have a drinks combination called the Boilermaker: a beer and a shot of whiskey. Having two drinks in front of you means you won't be under any pressure to accept a third. Also, it gives you an alibi when the shots start flying.

HOW TO ORDER A DRINK

In order to avoid a blank stare, looking like an idiot or a long and protracted conversation with a confused barman, there are three factors that should be considered when ordering a round of drinks.

1. WHAT IS THE BAR'S ATMOSPHERE?

Is it a tiki bar, grand hotel, cocktail club, members' club, speak easy, dive bar, pub or after hours place? If you get a chance do a bit of research before hand.

2. WILL THEY HAVE IT?

From here you'll be able to work out what they stock and the expertise of the barman.

3. WILL THE BARMAN KNOW HOW TO MAKE MY DRINK?

Think about how difficult your drink is to make, and how often the barman will have made it.

The Hierarchy of Drinks

In any major city there are roughly four levels of mixed drink you can order, starting from the basics (Gin and Tonic) to the mind-bendingly pretentious concoctions of molecular mixology.

1 THE BASICS

It is impossible to get these drinks wrong: Gin and Tonic, Whiskey and Coca-Cola – anything with one spirit and mixer. You can safely order these in a pub, sports bar or dive bar. The ice might not be fresh, the mixers might be flat, but it will still be drinkable.

2 THE CLASSICS

These are entry-level drinks every barman should know like the back of his hand: Martinis, Manhattans, Old Fashioneds and so on – but even so, you should tread carefully. Anywhere that serves 'house specials' will make a decent go of a classic cocktail. You're taking your

chances in a dive bar or an after-hours place. Avoid anything that requires fresh ingredients like lemon juice and drinks with more than three to four ingredients. Negronis, for instance, are hard to get wrong. It's just gin, vermouth and Campari in equal measure with ice. Even so, you will be amazed at how bad these can be sometimes.

3 LESSER-KNOWN CLASSICS

At this more intermediate level we are still in classic territory, but the drinks require more expertise and also the use of fresh ingredients. Sidecars, French 75s and Aviations are the kind of cocktails that the bar of a grand hotel or a members' club should be able to serve with ease. Do they have a large selection of bitters, whiskeys and brandies? If so, this will indicate that these

more interesting cocktails will be of a certain standard. The classics here are also usually spot-on.

The lesser-known cocktails are often made up of a slightly more adventurous mix than the classics. and can turn you into a more sophisticated drinker.

4 MOLECULAR MIXOLOGY

Look out for a barman using blenders, atomisers, nitrogen, sprays and fire. Also, places that use homemade bitters and syrups. Drinks-wise you'll be looking at stuff that involves flames, egg white and maybe even a spray of mist. Also, long-forgotten cocktails from Victorian times to the Prohibition era. As pretentious as these places can be sometimes, you can be sure all of the classics will be mixed with great panache.

Cocktail Drinking Tips

THEY'RE STRONG

A three-Martini lunch à la *Mad Men* may seem like a good idea. But if you're a cocktail novice it most certainly is not. It will get you very drunk, very quickly and in a manner that is entirely unpleasant. One every 45 minutes or so is about right.

BEFRIEND THE STAFF

Building up a rapport with the staff not only gets you better service, but also helps you to become a more accomplished cocktail drinker. Ask questions about their job, why they do things in a particular way or why they are using specific ingredients. If there is a bottle of spirits that you have not seen before, ask what it is.

WHAT TO WEAR

Focus on what is going on above the waist: a well-tailored jacket in a dark colour, a lightly coloured shirt, a simple textured tie and perhaps a pocket square to add flourish. This will be appropriate in most establishments. Show her that you have thought about what you're wearing. As Catherine Hayward, fashion director of *Esquire* advises, 'Thoughtful, but definitely not too try-hard.'

HOW TO GET SERVED

Attract the attention of the barman or table service with eye contact, a smile or an arched eyebrow. On no account wave money, click fingers or shout.

ORDERING FOR A FRIEND

Base your decision on the spirit they tend to drink. So a Manhattan if you've noticed they like whiskey. If they are novice drinkers suggest something light, refreshing and simple, like a Kir Royale or a Gin Fizz. Do not order strong cocktails for someone that isn't used to them.

Never order a drink for someone that you have never drunk before.

SEND IT BACK

If you like a drink served in a particular way ask politely, but don't be pedantic. A drink can be replaced or changed, if it is tasted, disliked and rejected immediately.

COCKTAIL ESSENTIALS

As with anything that requires a bit of kit – golf, espionage, sadomasochism etc – it is easy to get carried away with accumulating stuff, when all you really need is a few essentials, many of which you will already have in your kitchen. The point is to get mixing, drinking and drunk, not accumulate useless bits of ephemera. Here is a list of everything you need:

BOSTON SHAKER

Look for one with a metal top and a glass bottom. Glass conducts heat less effectively than metal and therefore will not dilute your drink as much.

BAR SPOON

Nothing wrong with just using a long spoon, chopstick or knife but looks the business, which adds to the fun.

SPIRIT MEASURE

This is also happily known as a jigger. Vital for making consistent drinks and also ones that combine several different kinds of booze and therefore require more accuracy.

POURER

An attachment you add to your bottles to control the flow of liquid.

JUICER

Preferably a non-mechanical one as these can break. Plastic ones have sharper ridges than glass ones.

A SHARP KNIFE

For the cutting, peeling and zesting of fruit.

BLUNT INSTRUMENT AND TEA TOWEL

For the bashing of ice, or for crushing fruit and herbs together

HAWTHORN STRAINER

Distinguished by a curved spring, this should fit flush onto the bottom part of your Boston Shaker.

AN ICE BUCKET

An insulated ice bucket will keep your ice nice and icy.

BLENDER

For puréeing fruit, for instance, peaches in a Bellini.

MIXING GLASS

A big plain glass for mixing and measuring drinks in.

GLASSES

For the millions of cocktails that exist, you only really need four types of glasses to cater for them all:

TUMBLER
For short iced drinks like Old Fashioned and Negroni.

HIGH BALL
For long iced drinks, like Gin and Tonic and Mojito.

CHAMPAGNE FLUTE
For champagne and champagne cocktails.

MARTINI GLASS
For chilled drinks that have no ice.

HOME BAR

For the basic home bar you should have these kinds of spirits:

1 **GIN**
It depends on your preference, some people like their gin to be quite fragrant, others dry. Plymouth, Tanqueray and Hendrick's are all perfectly good gins.

2 **VODKA**
Good vodka is good vodka, so Stolichnaya and Smirnoff, which are available practically everywhere are perfectly good.

3 **RUM**
With rum it's worth looking beyond Bacardi – try for something with extra body and kick to it. Specialty brands like Diplomatico have richer, more robust flavours while costing no more than Bacardi.

WHISKEY

4 There is no need to break out your 25-year-old malt whiskeys for cocktails. Good bourbon is not only cheaper, its robust flavours are generally more suited to making cocktails.

TEQUILA

5 Always have a good blanco or silver-grade tequila.

BRANDY

6 Brandy at its most rarified is expensive and unnecessary for good cocktails. A good VSOP cognac and Calvados will suffice.

BITTERS

7 A good bitter such as Campari and Aperol is essential to many cocktails. They are also great with sparkling wine. Always have a bottle of Angostura, Peychaud's and orange bitters handy.

OTHER INGREDIENTS

8 Finishing touches can make a great cocktail fantastic. Make sure you have a few of the following:

◆ Plenty of ice
◆ Sea salt
◆ Vermouth (Dolin or Noilly Prat)
◆ Fresh oranges, limes, lemons, grapefruit and fresh pinapple
◆ Sparkling mineral water
◆ Sparkling wine such as prosecco or cava
◆ A red and a white wine
◆ Tomato juice
◆ Maraschino cherries
◆ Green olives, pitted
◆ Syrup
◆ Grenadine
◆ Mineral water
◆ Club soda
◆ Tonic water
◆ Ginger beer and/or ale
◆ Cranberry juice
◆ Some basic liqueurs such as Bailey's, Amaretto and Cointreau

ANATOMY OF A GOOD COCKTAIL

What makes a good cocktail? Here is a short formula

FOOD

A cocktail should whet the appetite or aid digestion. All booze should really be enjoyed with food.

STRENGTH

Strong, but not too strong. It should not knock you out. Conversely, it should not have so much fizz and fruit that it tastes like an alcopop. You should be able to discern all of the different flavours of the different ingredients.

THE SENSES

It should look, smell, sound and taste nice. Good, fresh garnishes, the proper glasses chilled, high quality ingredients in their correct quantities and really icy bits of ice that crack and fizzle away.

COLD

Cocktails must be cooler than a polar bear's toenail and colder than an Eskimo's graveyard.

=

SPLENDID DRINK

You should look at it, smell it, and finally, drink it and think, 'Splendid!'

COCKTAIL TECHNIQUE

RELAX

Avoid any bar room acrobatics. It's just you making a nice drink for your friends.

ICE

You can never have enough. In addition to ice trays, simply fill up a plastic container to make one huge ice cube that you can chip away at.

GLASSES

Keep your cocktail glasses chilled.

HOME MADE SYRUP

It's just one part sugar and one part water, brought to the boil for 5 minutes. There's no need to buy it in. Also, avoid things like sour mix for Margaritas.

FRESH

Always use fresh fruit and herbs.

MUDDLING

Muddling is simply getting a blunt instrument to mash herbs so that they release their flavours.

MEASURE

Use your jigger. A cocktail is a careful balance of flavour and can use many ingredients, so measurements do matter.

SHAKING AND STIRRING

Just do as you're told. Shake when you're told to shake and stir when you're told to stir – it really does matter, and will make a difference to how your drink tastes.

TAKE CARE OF YOUR INGREDIENTS

Spirits stop aging after they have been bottled. However, they should only be kept for 6–8 months once opened and some, like Vermouth, need to be kept in the fridge.

▼

BLUFFER'S GUIDE TO WINE

If wine is your thing, then fine.
If not, there are basically only four kinds:

◆ Disgusting stuff that you get free at gallery openings and book launches. This is to be avoided at all costs. If there is beer at these events go for that instead, you'll thank yourself the next morning.
◆ OK stuff that you buy in the supermarket to have with dinner at

home. A little bit of research here and you might be able to sniff out a cheap bottle that's as tasty as an expensive bottle. But generally, you get what you pay for.
◆ Slightly nicer stuff you get in restaurants. Let's face it if you don't know anything about wine, this is

generally a bottle somewhere near the middle of the list. Read from left to right. You get what you pay for. If you're somewhere fancy, ask the wine waiter or sommelier what bargains there are or what they would recommend. Never ask the normal waiter.

◆ And finally, the amazing stuff from grand châteaux in France, like Pérus, Lafite Rothschild etc. Tasting one is like seeing a Picasso or a Dutch master for the first time. You finally get what the fuss is all about. These are the wines that turn normal drinkers into insufferable wine bores. But they really are worth the ritual and fuss. The memory stays with you for life.

WHAT TO DO

1 TASTE IT
Your wine can become 'corked' which means it's been infected with a fungus that makes it taste and smell like dust and mould. If they pour you a full glass and you've started drinking it, you're liable for the whole bottle.

2 GLASS
Drink wine in a wine glass – a glass with a wide mouth. This exposes the wine to air, helping to release more flavours.

3 SMELL IT
Wine smells nice! And it will reveal different fragrances and flavours as it warms up.

4 SIP IT
Sounds obvious, but don't slam it back. Sip it slowly and you can discern all of the different flavours that the wine is composed of.

5 CHECK IT
If a lesser vintage than the one you ordered has been brought to the table and

you have started drinking it, then you still pay for it. However, if you've accidently been given a superior one then you only pay for what you've ordered.

6 DON'T GURGLE

Gurgling and slurping is for your morning ablutions, not the dinner table.

7 KNOWLEDGE

Talking about vintages, tannins and fourth-generation producers when you know nothing will make you look stupid. The wine waiter, sommelier, or chap in the wine shop will be more than willing to help.

8 WINE, THEN FOOD

Make sure the wine gets to the table before the food.

9 IF YOU LIKE IT THEN IT'S GOOD

It's been scientifically proven that our enjoyment and appreciation of wine is greatly influenced by our expectations. While there is a huge difference between the blockbuster vintage wines and the plonk they serve at a gallery opening, the huge swathe of wines in the middle, are on the whole, a matter of personal preference.

10 GO BY THE LOOK OF THE LABEL

You know what? If it's got a French-looking label with old fonts and the word 'Château' written on it, then it probably is a classic French wine. And it'll probably be quite nice.

11 SPEND A BIT OF MONEY

In Britain, you're taking your chances with anything less than £10–15. In America, $20–30 and you can't really go wrong. You don't need to spend loads.

THE MAIN DIFFERENCE BETWEEN WHITE AND RED

White wine is an upper and makes you laugh a lot. Red wine makes you feel warm, content and sleepy. Fizzy white wine, such as prosecco, goes great with Aperol on a sunny day.

CHAMPAGNE

There are few occasions in life that cannot be improved with the liberal and regular application of champagne. And that includes hangovers, which you won't get if you only drink champagne. Keep a bottle or three in your fridge at all times. Even a dreary Wednesday afternoon in the office is a cause for celebration when there is champagne.

'TOO MUCH OF ANYTHING IS BAD, BUT TOO MUCH CHAMPAGNE IS JUST RIGHT.'

F. Scott Fitzgerald

Schmoozing

In business, fail to schmooze and prepare to lose.
Here's how to become the Machiavelli of Martinis and the
Sun Tzu of Singapore Slings.

SEDUCE THEM

Treat it like a date. Are they a man or a woman? How old are they? What kind of place are they going to want to go? And how are you going to get there? In many ways it is like a seduction. Prepare the ground and pay attention to the details as you would on a date.

MIRROR EFFECT

Match the venue to the values of the organisation. If you're trying to win business from Dunhill then somewhere like the Savoy is good. Less so if your client is easyJet. The same goes for drinks. Huge magnums of champagne will not impress people who work for Greenpeace, but will probably work for investment bankers.

SAY LESS THAN IS NECESSARY

Say as little as possible. Instead, listen. Psychologists have conducted tests to discover the kinds of people considered the most charming and interesting. It is always the person who speaks the least. Listening means that you are able to glean the vital piece of information, which could tip the balance in your favour.

DRINK LIKE THEM

Different countries have different drinking cultures. In South East Asia, someone who can drink a lot and participate in drinking games is generally considered quite impressive. Americans on the other hand drink very little.

HOW TO PARTY

IT'S A PARTY

Party! Have a dance! Tell a dirty story! Kiss a girl! But leave your political and religious convictions at home. Or anything else that is likely to cause confrontation for that matter. It's good to show you have an opinion, but avoid looking like a 'Mr know-it-all'. You'll simply look foolish.

TALK TO THE QUIET PERSON

Sometimes the most interesting person in the room is the quietest. This is probably because they are either supremely confident or supremely shy. The person that claims to be the life and soul of a party is often just loud and boorish.

TIPSY IS GOOD

Getting too drunk decreases your chances of having sex. Vomiting, falling asleep, getting into an argument or fight makes you look stupid. Too much drink also makes you loud and ignorant.

TIMING

It's rude to get there on time and it'll be boring. Get there after the pub shuts. And stay until the hosts start to get tired.

LIABILITIES

You can usually bring a guest, but make sure they aren't a liability. If they get too drunk, make inappropriate passes at married women, or are confrontational – it'll reflect badly on you.

GO ON YOUR OWN
Going to parties on your own shows a lot of confidence and forces you to talk to new people.

BRING SOMETHING
Bring something to drink, but on no account take it home with you if it isn't drunk on the night. Champagne is always welcome.

PARTY HOPPING
Give the party a chance before moving on.

IF IN DOUBT, OVERDRESS
Overdressing is sexy. And it makes you look as though you've somewhere better to go.

THE OFFICE PARTY

Ah, who doesn't enjoy organised, enforced fun? Here's how to get through it without getting the sack.

YOU HAVE TO GO
Short of hospitalisation or the death of a close relative, there's no way of getting out of it.

IT'S STILL WORK
According to employment legislation you can get the sack for any misconduct that takes place at

the office party. So think twice before making a pass at that hot intern. Don't do anything you wouldn't do during normal office hours.

SOCIAL MEDIA

Executives should declare either a ban or an amnesty on social networking and photo taking during the office party. But they won't. Tweeting something offensive while drunk at the office party has gotten people the sack before.

NEVER ARRIVE ON TIME

Arrive on time and it'll be you and Dave from IT eating vol-au-vents. Alone. Someone will put on 'Gangnam Style'. The disco lights will spin. The mumsy woman from HR will get out the mistletoe. You wipe away a tear.

DON'T BE TOO COOL

You might discover Dave is actually quite a nice guy. Hey, you might even realise that your job isn't so bad after all.

EAT BEFORE YOU GET THERE

The food will be rubbish. And you'll be drinking. So at least have a snack before you get there.

TAKE IT EASY

Attacking the free bar like a desert nomad at an oasis is going to end badly. Drinking at the office party is to be approached with causion.

AFTER PARTY

Have an after-hours drink somewhere far away from the office party with colleagues you genuinely like.

THE AFTERMATH

Try to get in on time the next day.

Apologise to anyone you need to apologise to sincerely, discretely and swiftly.

How to party headline

You only have to get it right once. The kudos achieved by throwing one legendary party will ensure your popularity for many years to come.

WHAT IS A GOOD PARTY?

One in which bad things happen. Lewd jokes, wanton lechery, confessions, dirty dancing, break-ups, make-ups, fleeting embraces and stolen kisses. You don't want a forgettable evening of nibbles and drinks. You want something that teeters constantly on the edge of chaos.

THE GUEST LIST

Opposites not only attract, they also create positive energy. Especially when they've got a few drinks inside them. Get the fashion PR into a conversation with the atomic scientist, the banker with the suburban hairdresser, and see what happens. You want a combination of people who know each other and people who don't.

TAKE THE PARTY HOME

Gather a group of friends and go to your favourite bar first. This means you are not sat around at home waiting for the party to start in dribs and drabs. Instead, you are bringing it back home with you and making it start with a bang.

RANDOMS

Just as a good Bloody Mary needs a bit of kick and spice to it, so too, does your party. When you are at the bar get one of your female companions to befriend a group of attractive girls (strangers) and invite them to your party.

DJ

Get a DJ in. Don't just fiddle around on a computer. A good DJ actually doing some mixing adds to the sense of occasion. Make them play party music – The Rolling Stones, Jay-Z, Michael Jackson, Rick James – nothing too cool or niche.

TEAM EFFORT

As a host you want to be busy having a good time and introducing people to one another. Assign several trusted male friends with some of the other tasks.

FOOD

Nobody has ever remembered a party for the food. They remember them for who had sex with whom and who confessed something they shouldn't have. So don't get too carried away, as nobody will care. At the very least provide posh crisps. At the most get your local restaurant to prepare some snacks.

PARTY CHECKLIST

1 Slice lemons and limes beforehand. Drunkards with blades ruin parties.

2 Parsimony is an absolutely unforgivable. Get as much alcohol as possible.

3 Get as much ice as possible and then double it.

4 Get an interesting-looking receptacle. A traditional baby's pram filled with ice makes a good champagne cooler.

5 Pre-chill as many glasses as possible. Get extra ones in.

6 Dress code – don't be too specific, but try to make sure everyone has made some kind of effort, men especially.

7 Scented candles will make even the drabbest flat look like a place in which seduction can take place.

8 Don't forget to prepare the outside. Get heaters, garden furniture and lanterns.

9 Don't try to prepare everyone a cocktail. Instead provide ingredients and equipment for people to make their own and make punches.

10 If all else fails hire your favourite bar tender to do everything.

DINNER PARTY

Dinner is important but not as important as a good time. You are not a Michelin-starred chef and your friends are not going to expect you to cook like one. The more time you spend fussing in the kitchen and fretting about plating up, the less time you're spending being a good host.

HERE'S HOW TO MAKE IT EASY ON YOURSELF:

◆ Stick to one country: if you're making a pasta dish as your main course, complement it with Italian side dishes and salads. Keep it consistent. This will make planning the menu and cooking much easier.

◆ Keep the dishes simple and do as much cooking in advance as possible.

◆ Variety is key: a meat or fish, a salad or vegetable, something spicy, something sweet. Balance is important too. A creamy dessert after lasagne is going to be too heavy.

◆ Not everything has to be homemade. The local deli can save you lots of time.

◆ Cook big dishes that can be brought out at the same time. Let people serve themselves. Avoid any complex plating up manoeuvres and choose food that can be served warm.

◆ Cook enough, but there's no need to put a Roman banquet on.

Dancing

**Dancing (well) gets you laid.
Women equate dancing with sex and science
has proved it. But let's face it, we're all pretty useless
on the dance floor.**

KEEP IT SIMPLE

Cut out all the hip-hop gesticulations and booty grinding. You are not 'stepping up 2 da street' – you are desperately trying to avoid embarrassment. You're not Mick Jagger either. Or John Travolta. All of these are tempting if you don't dance much, but try to resist. Aim for a cool, rhythmic strut.

THE STEP-TOUCH

The step-touch is the move Will Smith teaches in *Hitch* and it's fool proof. Even if you're not the best of movers, you can definitely master these three simple steps.

1. Step with your right: 'Step' and bring your left leg to the right: 'touch.'
2. Repeat in the opposite direction.
3. If you want a bit of variety, try snapping your fingers or doing the odd clap in time to the music

DON'T GURN LIKE A LOON

Aim for a look of cool detachment. Keep your lips and eyebrows under control. Leave your tongue in your mouth and your orgasm face in the bedroom. Nobody needs to see this. Practice your dance moves infront of a mirror if you have to.

STAY SHARP

The beauty of the step-touch is that you don't move around too much, meaning you won't get too sweaty. Don't be the sweaty, gurning loon, doing the electric slide with his tie at halfmast and shirt un-tucked.

AND IF YOU CAN DANCE

If you have been blessed with the feet of Fred Astaire be gracious. Chances are, you're only a good dancer in your head. In any case, women treat men who dance well with suspicion.

IGNORE ALL OF THIS

Just dance like no-one is watching. It's a party isn't it?!

HOW TO SLOW DANCE

She smiled, so you smiled back. Now she's laughing at your jokes. She likes *Curb Your Enthusiasm* and you like *Curb Your Enthusiasm*. Wow! You have studiously avoided dancing all night. But somehow both have managed to drift onto the dance floor. The music just got turned off. Phew. But what's this? It's started up again. Slow dance. Oh no...

1 TAKE CONTROL

If there isn't any way of getting out of it, take control of the situation. Don't act as though you need to be cajoled into dancing with her. Confidently lead her onto the dance floor. Say, 'Baby, there's nothing to worry about'. Slow and smooth, my son. Slow and smooth.

2 DON'T LOOK AT YOUR FRIENDS

You might have some immature friends guffawing away in the background. You have her in your arms right. She smells nice. She's just as nervous as you are. Who wants to dance with them? Exactly.

GET INTO POSITION

3

Position her so that your heads are about a foot or two away from each other. The position of your foot is key here. Either have your feet offset: each other's right foot inside the other's pair. Or just have her feet in the middle of yours. A toe-to-toe foot stance is martial, so avoid that. At this point she might even place her arms around your neck.

INTIMACY

4

Err on the safe side. Put your right hand on the left side of her hip and use your left to gently hold her right hand, which should be at her shoulder height. She can put her left on your shoulder. This is a basic ballroom stance. If it's going well you might want to try putting your hand on her waist.

LEAD

5

Try to do it with subtlety and grace. Gently indicate where you want her to go. Moving her around like a mop is not going to get you very far. No dipping either.

KISS! KISS! KISS!

6

Let's face it; if you fancy each other, a slow dance is not really about dancing. It's an opportunity to gently turn up the intimacy between two prospective lovers. Look her in the eye, smile your nicest smile and tell her how beautiful she looks. Then plant one kiss her lips.

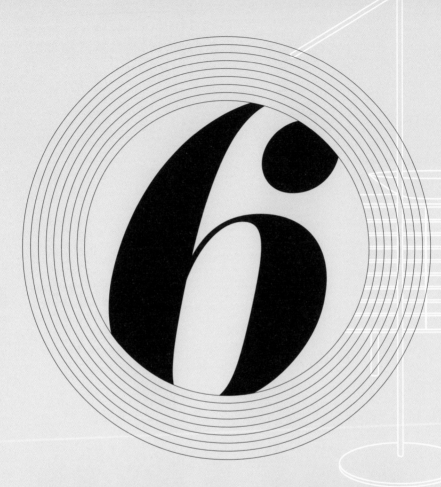

SEDUCTION

WITH DOUG HAINES,
CO-FOUNDER OF THE LONDON SCHOOL OF ATTRACTION

The Ten Biggest Mistakes Men Make

***Here are ten common mistakes men make
when they try to find love.***

1 NOT APPROACHING

There's nothing creepier than a guy who just hangs around, looks over and DOESN'T approach. Women want you to come over; they want the cut and thrust of some interesting conversation and they want some bravery.

2 TRYING AND FAILING TO BE COCKY

A gentle and funny tease shows that you aren't so in awe of her you can't have fun. Done badly, however, a tease can come across as an insult. So if you think her hat looks absurd, tell her with a smile and keep the intonation gentle. Blurting out, 'What a rubbish hat' is to be avoided.

3 OVERDOING THE ALCOHOL

No woman wants a gibbering drunk approaching her.

4 IGNORING HER FRIEND

Don't make the cardinal sin of ignoring her friend. Act like a gentleman and regale both women with your charm. Homing in on only one of them is rude, will alienate her friend and ultimately see you kicked to the curb.

5 TRYING TO BE JAMES BOND

If you're a suave, well-dressed, Bentley-driving charmer of international renown, you can afford to act as such. If you're a slightly nervous computer programmer, trying to pull the wool over her eyes is futile. True confidence means accepting who you are and being that person without apology.

6 THINKING TOO MUCH ABOUT WHAT TO SAY

A sure-fire way to lose your train of thought is to ask yourself what to say. Instead, focus your thoughts on walking over and saying hello. Then just open your mouth and start talking: about your day; about what you're doing; about what she's wearing; about why you noticed her; about the bar. Whatever it is, don't worry about 'what' to say.

7 LIMITING YOURSELF

Approximately 99.9 per cent of men follow the rules; the rules that ordain we may only talk to women in pre-designated areas such as bars, at a friend's party or an online dating forum. Don't limit yourself by these pointless rules; if you see a beautiful woman walking down the street, go over and say hello. Confidence is key, but be careful not to come across as cocky. There is nothing wrong with saying hello. In fact, she'll find it flattering.

8 ASKING TOO MANY QUESTIONS

We're told that showing an interest in others is polite. This is true, but only once you've made a connection with that person. If you walk up to a girl and start asking her questions – without first building some rapport – she'll be reluctant to respond. Don't interview her; keep it light-hearted and have something to say.

9 OBSESSING OVER ONE WOMAN

You've been talking for over an hour. You're getting along well and you're falling for her. But then the night takes a new turn, you lose her and your night is ruined. The problem: you're not approaching enough women and so you're becoming emotionally attached to someone you've just met. You need to meet a lot of women so you don't become too invested in one. Keep your options open and talk to a few different women.

10 BLAMING YOURSELF

If the woman at the bar brushes you off, or the date goes badly, don't take it on the chin. Don't blame yourself and wonder what you did wrong. If things aren't going well, it's a good thing: it means you're making an effort. As Winston Churchill once said, 'If you're going through hell, keep going'.

HOW TO ASK A WOMAN OUT

It's natural to feel nervous before approaching a woman. But surely, that's part of the fun?

The worst course of action is no action. So shoot your cuffs, straighten your tie and smooth your hair own, it's time to sweep her off her feet.

FIRST THINGS FIRST

Are you well dressed? A man in a nice suit always turns heads. Do you smell nice? Are you well groomed? Make sure you've had a shave or that your facial hair is looking neat and tidy. Another overlooked detail is fingernails.

They need to be trimmed and clean. Women notice these things because they put so much effort into making themselves beautiful.

DIRECT

The temptation would be to pussyfoot about, but now is the time to be bold. Just be honest. Tell her that she's caught your eye. A well-timed complement would work here but make it specific to the woman: 'You look amazing in that dress' not 'I love your dress'.

RAPPORT

Firing off a volley of questions like an integrator will make her feel awkward. Instead, offer something of yourself: tell her interesting stories, notice the nuances of the world around her and engage her in a conversation – emotions, thoughts and feelings rather than cold facts.

SEED THE DATE

When you're sharing a funny story, work in an opportunity to see each other again. For instance, if you both love fin de siècle French painting, you say: 'Oh, there's a Fragonard exhibition on at the Wallace Collection.' Her: 'Oh really?' Sell the date a little bit before asking her out. Tell her what a beautiful place Hertford House is, that there's a knock out Oliver Peyton restaurant there etc. If done properly, she may even ask you out.

CLOSE

Never just ask for her number out of the blue. only once you've established the reason for seeing each other again. In fact, you've sold the date well and built up a good rapport, you may find that she gives you her number without prompting. It's all about communication. Give her a reason to want to see you again.

DON'T LIMIT YOURSELF

Do not confine your efforts to bars and nightclubs. These are not the only places to meet women or even the best place to get to know them. You will see women walking around the streets, in coffee shops and at your local supermarket. Be brave and say hello – the man who does this one hundred times will change his life.

Online Dating

With the wrong approach online dating can be laborious and unfruitful. Here's how to make it worth your while.

REAL LIFE

Are you sure you're not better off approaching women in real life? It's much more fun and less time consuming. Even if you don't like bars and clubs, your local high street, bookshops, coffee shops – all of these are much better places to try your luck than online. However, if you must, Doug Haines from the London School of Attraction will show you how.

DATING PROFILE

The purpose of an online dating profile isn't to tell the girl what you're like; it's to tell the girl what you want.

In doing so, you demonstrate:

1. STANDARDS
You're not just going to go out with the first girl who shows an interest in you

2. DISCERNMENT
You've thought about what you're looking for. You've thought about what sort of girls you're compatible with and what kind of people you like to spend time with.

3. HIGH VALUE
You're a catch and you expect a girl to bring plenty to the table.

HOW NOT TO DO IT

Avoid bland, generic stuff like:

1. I'm looking for a girl who doesn't take herself too seriously.

2. I'd love to meet a woman who stays in shape.

3. A good sense of humour is really important to me.

What kind of woman would define herself as a crabby slob who takes herself seriously? Exactly.

HOW TO DO IT PROPERLY

To get your online dating profile to sparkle, throw in something that gets attention.

Come up with something that girls will love and hate:

♦ You must love cricket
♦ You must hate Spanish music
♦ You must prefer cats to dogs

Make it fun and make her laugh. Give her something to think and write about when she replies.

SHOW, DON'T TELL

Don't just say that you're funny, write a joke or tell a funny story. Don't say that you're sporty. Instead include a picture of you playing some sport. This is a far more powerful way to communicate.

FIRST MESSAGE

Online dating is a numbers game. You have to send out a high volume of messages to get a small number of dates. Girls on dating sites will be sceptical and most girls will receive a high volume of messages – yours must stand out.

PRINCIPLES BEHIND A GOOD FIRST MESSAGE:

QUALIFICATION

Create a message which asks the girl to prove herself to you. She'll have loads of messages from guys all telling her what a great time she'd have with him. Make her take notice by flipping this dynamic. Instead of 'If we go out we'll have a great time because I'm really funny' say, 'I wonder if you'd be funny enough for me to take you out'.

KEEP IT SHORT

An essay tells her that you place a very high importance on her reply, and that you have nothing better to do than sit at home constructing long emails to girls you've never met. Keep the message short.

ENGAGE HER

Ask questions which she needs to answer correctly to get a date with you. This works because it gives her something to do, something to think about and allows for a creative reply. Or ask her opinion on something: 'I have sponsored an elephant in India for my niece and I need to give it a name – what do you think?'

COMPLIMENT HER

Ideally you would compliment every girl about something specific on her profile. However, it's difficult to personalise a high volume of messages. The extra effort to include a personalised compliment is not worth the time – a generic 'cute picture' works just as well.

TELL HER WHAT IS HAPPENING

A message with no obvious goal can seem annoying and pointless for a girl when she is online dating. If you are giving her a little test to see whether she can 'earn' a date, tell her this. Don't just send a get-to-know-you message. Articulate an end game and a purpose to the message, even if it's just that you liked her.

SUBJECT LINE

The average good-looking girl will get dozens of messages every day. On most sites all she sees is the subject line. If it has the subject line 'hello' it will simply be lost in the sea of all the other messages. In all likelihood, it won't even be opened.

GET HER ATTENTION

It must stand out. It doesn't matter if it stands out because it's funny, clever or even rude. It simply must catch her eye among all those 'hi' and 'hello' subjects.

DISQUALIFY YOURSELF

A great way to stand out is to disqualify yourself in the subject line. Rather than, 'We'd be great together' say 'This is NOT going to work'. Disqualifying yourself shows that you're not taking the online dating thing very seriously (always a good idea).

ALLOW THE SUBJECT LINE TO FLOW INTO YOUR MESSAGE

Start a sentence in the subject line and then finish it in the first line of the message proper. Something like 'Hey I wanted to tell you...'

JUST WRITE SOMETHING RANDOM IF YOU GET STUCK

Just write the first thing that comes to mind. Look around you – what can you see? It sounds stupid, but whatever you just thought of is a million times better than 'Hello'. Even if it's 'A blue stapler that doesn't really work'.

POSE SIMPLE QUESTIONS

However lame they are, it's human nature to want to answer questions. If you can't think of anything clever, just write whatever is on your mind. *The Wire* or *Sopranos*? is on my mind right now.

DATING

A good date needs to get off to a strong start.

HOW NOT TO DO IT

A good date needs to get off to a strong start. This is how the first five minutes of a typical bad date go from a girl's perspective:

◆ Guy greets her nervously at the station.

◆ He asks her what she's been up to.

◆ They walk to the bar without touching.

◆ He asks her a succession of boring questions.

◆ At the bar he says 'What would you like?'

◆ They sit down and continue the small talk.

FIRST FIVE MINUTES ARE CRUCIAL

It is almost impossible to recover from a bad opening five minutes. If she feels uncomfortable and awkward at the start, she's unlikely to warm up later.

AVOID HAIRDRESSER CONVERSATION

Hairdresser conversation is the inane pleasantries you exchange before they cut your hair. And it will kill a date.

◆ How are you?

◆ How was your day?

◆ What have you been up to?

- How's work?

- Did you get here ok?

- Have you been here before?

They're bad enough when asked them by someone you know: they don't generate interesting conversation and they're lazy. They're also quite difficult to decide how to answer – you've been up to a lot of things recently, which ones should you talk about if you want to impress? She's far too nervous to be able to give interesting answers.

A Good Date

OFFER YOUR ARM
Touch her right away. Smile confidently and give her a big hug when you meet her. Then, as you start walking towards wherever you're going, offer her your elbow so you can walk arm in arm. By the time you get to the bar, you'll both be comfortable with touching each other and you'll have surprised her with a touch of old-fashioned gallantry.

STORY
Launch into a story, anecdote or observation. It doesn't even have to be exciting. As long as you deliver it with some expression and passion you can talk about anything. This is the one time when it's you that needs to be doing all the talking.

LET HER RELAX

If you start with a story she can chill out, get comfortable and listen to you without any pressure to come up with something interesting herself.

REMIND HER WHO YOU ARE

The first time you met this girl might have only been for a few minutes, or she might have had a few drinks when you did meet. Give her a minute or two to remember who you are, what you're like, what your voice sounds like and why she liked you in the first place.

LET HER KNOW YOU'RE A NORMAL GUY

Girls can be very suspicious of guys and, by filling in a little of your backstory, you can 'normalise' yourself. Any time you mention something about a friend, your job, a family member, a book

you're reading you become a bit more 'real' in her eyes.

GIVE HER LOTS OF CONVERSATIONAL HOOKS

She'll often be worried about having enough to talk about. When you tell a story, within a few minutes you'll have given her dozens of things to ask you about or comment on.

CONVEY SOME HUMOUR

This is less important than making her feel comfortable, but it can't hurt at this stage to show that you're a cool guy with a (self-deprecating) sense of humour.

GET THE ENERGY OF THE DATE RIGHT

Good dates are all about energy. Telling a story will get you chatting, agreeing, arguing, reminiscing anything is better than hairdresser conversation.

LET HER KNOW THAT YOU'RE IN CHARGE

Girls want a guy who can lead and take care of them. If you start by asking questions, you're asking her to lead; just start talking and she'll relax in the knowledge that she's with a man who can handle these things.

CHEERS

If you live in a major city there is no excuse for chain bars and restaurants. Choose somewhere unique. Go where you're likely to bump into acquaintances and friends that won't embarrass you. For instance, if you know the owner of a good restaurant, go there. If he can give you a bit of special treatment, a good table, a new dish or cocktail to try out, even better.

SEVERAL VENUES

Have different venues lined up. If you go to two or three different places on a date the girl will feel like she has known you for longer and will also keep the date interesting. For example, going from a quirky coffee shop to an intimate wine bar via an arcade will work well. The coffee shop is nice for getting to know each other in a non-intimidating way; the arcade will be more playful and fun and the cocktail bar will be a romantic conclusion where you can be more seductive.

DON'T PUT ALL YOUR EGGS IN ONE BASKET

You will feel pressure on a date if it is the only date in your diary. Try to fill up your week with as many dates and cool stuff as possible so the date seems less important. You can't magic dates ex nihilo, but try to arrange meeting with friends. The more you have on, the more relaxed you will feel on the date.

SURPRISE HER

The girl has been on hundreds of dates. She has a blueprint of what she will be expecting and, even if you deliver this 'standard date' really well, it is unlikely to be memorable. So mix it up: take her somewhere unusual, leave when it's going well or pretend you're expecting her to lead, when actually you have planned it all along. An element of surprise is a good tool for keeping it interesting.

KNOW HOW TO KISS HER

A lot of guys struggle with this area. Lunging in for the kiss unexpectedly has got disaster written all over it. Build up the kiss slowly by increasing the sexual intensity of your physical touches and eye contact so that a kiss becomes inevitable:

1. A touch on the arm.
2. Holding hands.
3. Arm around her shoulder/waist.
4. Whispering into her ear.
5. Kissing her.

There are cheeky and easy ways to bring the kiss to the fore without the need to lunge. As you are talking, slip this in: 'Sorry to interrupt – just wanted to tell you that I'm going to kiss you in a few minutes. Now what were you saying? Her reaction will tell you whether this is on the cards!

Or be a bit more romantic: 'I'm sorry, I wasn't listening to a word you were saying- I was just thinking about kissing you. You were saying your boss is annoying...' These strategies allow you to gauge her reaction and build sexual tension without risking everything on a lunge. She'll be so impressed that she may even be the first one to make the move!

Don't think the hard work is done once the first date is secured. Appreciate it has only just begun and go prepared.

HOW TO GET
THE SHAG PAD READY

A carefully planned seduction can come undone if your place isn't up to scratch.

CONDOMS
Have them in ample supply. There's no need to keep them in a jar by the bedside table, but they need to be there somewhere.

MUSIC
Your penchant for obscure soundtracks or blood-curdling drum-and-bass won't cut it here. Obvious stuff is fine – Marvin Gaye, D'Angelo and anything Motown. Have it ready to play as soon as you get in, instead of having to wait for a laptop to fire up.

OLD CLOTHES
You will have accumulated a collection of oversized T-shirts and items of clothing you don't wear anymore. Don't give her your cornflower blue Charvet shirt. You'll never see it again. Unless of course, you really like her.

FRIDGE
Keep a bottle of champagne or sparkling wine in your fridge. Failing that, something white. Girls generally prefer white wine. Some breakfast wouldn't go amiss either.

BATHROOM
By most female standards your bathroom will be disgusting. It'll never be as clean as hers, but try at least, to make it less disgusting. Make sure that it smells fresh at all times.

EVIDENCE

Ruthlessly expunge any evidence of masturbatory bachelordom. No one has pornographic magazines and DVDs anymore, but have you cleared the search history on your laptop? Tear down any pin-up calenders and posters, even if they are supposed to be 'ironic'.

SHEETS

Invest in good bed linen. Buying 5-star hotel quality bed linen is some of the best money you will ever spend. She'll appreciate the smell and feel of soft, freshly laundered four hundred-thread count Egyptian cotton. Your He-Man sheets won't be

FLATMATES

Tell them to go away. Or at least get them to behave. Let them know you will be bringing back company.

OTHER WOMEN

Don't have pictures of other women lying around. No trace evidence of previous lovers either: lingerie, lipsticks etc. She really won't be impressed.

LIGHTING

Soft light, candles, dimmer switches are key if she's going to sleep with a stranger.

THE JOY OF SEXT

Sexting is no longer confined to hormone-addled teenagers who live to regret it. Nor is it solely the dirty secret of politicians who should know better. At some point, if you want to have sex with her, you'll be called upon to craft a dirty little five-word bon mot at four in the morning. Here's how to do it safely.

1 GET TO THE POINT

As with all good writing, sexts need to get straight to the point. That way you avoid being entered for a Bad Sex Award, which is a British literary prize awarded to novelists for embarrassing sex scenes. You want her imagination to do the hard work, ahem, so to speak.

2 MAKE IT UP AS YOU GO ALONG

You don't need to tell the truth. If she asks whether you're wearing the bespoke suit she finds you irresistible in. Say yes and ask her what she's wearing. Don't tell her you're in your Spider-Man pyjamas.

3 NO PICS

You know how we said show never tell when writing a dating profile? It doesn't apply in this case.

A gentleman never ever shows her naked pictures of him or shows his friends naked pics that he's been sent by a lady.

4 START SLOW

Gently turn the heat up, especially if you don't know them very well.

5 UH OH

It is quite possible to know several Sarahs and Kates. Make sure you have sent it to the right one.

6 IT'S HOT AND STUPID

Done right, sexting can be as hot as the real thing, but in the cold light of day the messages will make you look like an idiot. If she goes round showing people your sexts just laugh it off. And of course, you must never do such a thing yourself.

INDEX

R

razors 34

S

T

ALFRED TONG

was born in London in 1978 and has lived in South
London, Essex, Los Angeles and Hong Kong.
He studied Journalism at the London College of
Fashion and has written for *The Times*, *Esquire* and
Time Out London. This is his second book.

JACK HUGHES

was born during the summer of '89 in Croydon, South
London. He studied illustration at Kingston University
and now lives in Chiswick, West London.
He is the in-house fashion illustrator at *ShortList*
magazine for 'Mr Hyde'; the daily email for men.
He has previously illustrated for *ELLE*, Harrods,
Burberry and *Wired*.

Acknowledgements

Thanks to Kate Pollard
and Kajal Mistry at Hardie Grant,
Jack Hughes for his stylish
illustrations and Matt Phare for the
brilliant design work.

The Gentleman's Handbook by Alfred Tong

First published in 2013 by Hardie Grant Books
This revised edition published in 2017 by Hardie Grant Books

Hardie Grant Books (UK)
52-54 Southwark Street
London SE1 1UN
hardiegrant.com

Hardie Grant Books (Australia)
Ground Floor, Building 1
658 Church Street
Melbourne, VIC 3121
hardiegrant.com

The moral rights of Alfred Tong to be identified as the author of this work have been asserted
by him in accordance with the Copyright, Designs and Patents Act 1988.

Text © Alfred Tong
Illustrator © Jack Hughes

All rights reserved. No part of this publication may be reproduced,
stored in a retrieval system or transmitted in any form by any
means, electronic, electrostatic, magnetic tape, mechanical,
photocopying, recording or otherwise, without
the prior written permission of the Publisher.

British Library Cataloguing-in-Publication Data. A catalogue record
for this book is available from the British Library.

ISBN: 978-1-78488-138-2

Publisher: Kate Pollard
Senior Editor: Kajal Mistry
Editorial Assistant: Hannah Roberts
Publishing Assistant: Eila Purvis
Illustrator: Jack Hughes
Art Direction and Design: Matt Phare
Colour Reproduction by p2d

Printed and bound in China by 1010

10 9 8 7 6 5 4 3 2 1